100
NIGHTS AT THE OPERA
WEXFORD FESTIVAL OPERA
AN ANTHOLOGY

100 NIGHTS AT THE OPERA

AN ANTHOLOGY
TO CELEBRATE THE 40TH ANNIVERSARY OF THE
WEXFORD FESTIVAL OPERA

EDITED BY IAN FOX

TOWN
HOUSE

Published in 1991 by
Town House and Country House
42 Morehampton Road
Donnybrook Dublin 4

British Library Cataloguing in Publication Data available

ISBN: 0-948524-32-4

Acknowledgements
The publishers would like to thank the following for photographic
material:

Denis O'Connor, pp 10, 41, 43, 91, 92, 94, 97 (Otello), 98, 99
(Mayor of Loxford), 102, 103 (*Il Re Pastore* and Vivian Martin),
126; The Royal Opera House, Covent Garden, p 18 (David
Fielding); Christopher Hunt Ltd, p 18 (Brian Dickie); Gillian Smith,
p 19 (Heskett Piano Trio); John Coast, p 20 (Dennis O'Neill); Bord
Fáilte Éireann, pp 21 (Thomson Smillie), 23 (exhibition photo), 37,
55 (Ballyhack), 90 (Veronica Dunne et al), 97 (Lucia di
Lammermoor), 120; Als Management Ltd, London, p 24 (Patrick
Libby); Guy Gravett, p 33 (Myer Fredman); Wilfred C Stiff, p 38
(Bryan Balkwill); The National Gallery of Ireland, p 58; John
Ironside, pp 81-84, 114, 115 (*Königskinder*); Amelia Stein, pp
85-88; E Piccagliani, Teatro alla Scala, p 95 (Aldo Ceccato); Jean
Pierre Leloir, p 95 (Theodor Guschlbauer); Harrison/Farott Ltd,
London, p 100 (Felicity Palmer); Photo Musica, Middlesex, p 100
(Gill Gomez); Fred Runeberg, p 110 (Petteri Salomaa); Eric
Thorburn, p 107 (David Pountney); Music International, London, p
115 (Joan Davies); The Clarion Musical Society, New York, p 115
(Newell Jenkins); Clive Boursnell and *The Sunday Times,* p 131;
The Irish Times, p 134.

All archival material courtesy of The Wexford Festival Opera.
Special thanks to the County Librarian, Wexford, for assistance
with the archives.

Cover photo: from *The Rising of the Moon* (1990)

Managing editor: Treasa Coady
Text editor: Elaine Campion
Text and cover design: Bill Murphy
Colour origination: The Kulor Centre
Typeset by Printset & Design Ltd, Dublin
Printed in Ireland by Criterion Press, Dublin

Contents

Foreword

It has long been one of Wexford's ambitions to publish a book about the Wexford Festival Opera. The initial plan was to publish a definitive history.

Tentative approaches to prospective authors and publishers soon made it abundantly clear that an assortment of mouldy files, some equally damp books of press cuttings, and enthusiastic rather than optimistic mutterings about the 'wealth of material' that many people must have, did not constitute an archive. And without an archive no author could undertake such a book.

So, Wexford wanted an archive. Due to the generosity and co-operation of the local authority and the county librarian, room was made available in the County Library at Wexford. Soon material began to arrive, as people who did indeed have material confidently placed it in the safe keeping of the library staff. Yet however safe the venue and important the material, no 'would be' author could afford the time to sort it out in order to extract the necessary information.

Wexford wanted an archivist. Now archivists and their assistants do not grow on trees and as everyone knows, Wexford never has money for such luxuries. It was suggested to FÁS, who were seeking a suitable project as a contribution to the local community, that an archive for the Wexford Festival might be acceptable, especially as it was their fortieth anniversary. And so this worthwhile work has been started.

But Wexford still wanted a book. And it was clear that it would be some time before the archive would be of sufficient help to an author intent on writing a serious history. What about a coffee-table book they asked, and would it require a lot of money or research?

The fact that in 1991 you hold in your hand a book from the Wexford Festival Opera to mark its fortieth anniversary, is in itself an example of the tenacity that epitomises Wexford. A refusal to accept 'no'.

People of the calibre of Ian Fox (editor), Treasa Coady (publisher) and many other eminent contributors responded to a request for help. Indeed they not only agreed to help but made it abundantly clear that such was their affection and regard for Wexford that they considered it an honour and a pleasure to assist. Wexford is indebted to them.

Barbara Wallace
Chairman

Preface

It begins as a slight ache in the right elbow and then becomes a stabbing pain along the arm; it doesn't come from heaving large opera scores around, but is the result of having one's arm twisted via the telephone, in the gentlest possible way, by a Wexford Festival enthusiast. John Small is one of the past masters of the art. 'A little book, a souvenir of the fortieth year, a few articles, some pictures... you know what to do'. There are only two courses of action: either say 'sorry, you have the wrong number', or give in. The latter course is the less dangerous. Soon I was wading through heaps of photographs, enormous scrapbooks, dusty files and all the diverse material of the Festival, which at last has found a home at the County Library. There the Festival's first archivist is starting the daunting task of putting some shape on the huge amount of disorganised material from the past. It is not feasible to contemplate a formal history until this mammoth operation is over, but meanwhile there is room for a substantial memoir of the Festival's first forty years.

It is a remarkable story by any standards. An enormous amount has already been written about the Festival, in reviews, in books, as tourist articles, in the Festival's programmes. In this volume we have tried to give something of the flavour of this material. Reminiscences of the early days, a diversity of views, a little musicology, lots of pictures and the full cast lists of the 104 operas which have been staged up to 1990. In fact one opera, *Don Pasquale,* appeared twice, and on three occasions there have been double or triple bills on the same evening, so with a little miscalculation I could claim that we are celebrating 100 operatic nights — it makes a better title anyhow!

I must thank a number of people who have helped minimise our race against the clock in bringing this book to you for the fortieth anniversary — the committee (should I say 'gang') of three who had the idea: John Small, James O'Connor and Niall McConnell, our indefatigable chairman Barbara Wallace, Jerome Hynes and his ever-helpful team, archivist John MacArdle, Kathrine Lucking and the County Library, and all those who helped the project unhesitatingly. In particular I must thank our contributors, who so generously allowed their writings to appear without any personal gain so that the Festival's eternal financial problems could be helped a little. Indeed, if their words inspire you to do that little bit more for this great Festival, you can make sure that as many copies as possible are purchased! You will also make our unflappable and inspiring publisher, Treasa Coady, a little less anxious!

Ian Fox
Editor

Festival Folk

Dr Des Ffrench, Sir Compton Mackenzie, Mrs Walsh and Dr Tom Walsh at the reopening of the theatre in 1961.

Festival Folk

Presidents

1951-1972 Compton MacKenzie
1974-1976 Lauder Greenway
1977-   Alfred Beit

Chairmen

1951-1955 Tom Walsh
1956-1961 Fr M J O'Neill
1962-1966 Alfred Beit
1967-1970 Dr J D Ffrench
1971-1976 Seán Scallan
1977-1979 Brigadier Richard Jefferies
1980-1985 Jim Golden
1986-   Barbara Wallace

Artistic Directors

1951-1966 Tom Walsh
1967-1973 Brian Dickie
1974-1978 Thomson Smillie
1979-1981 Adrian Slack
1982-   Elaine Padmore

katya   oberon   gualtiero

tichon   fatima   gerasmin   boris

kabanicha   imogene   huon

rezia   puck   ernesto

Wexford Festival Council 1991

Patrons	The Right Reverend Noel V Willoughby, BD Bishop of Cashel, Ferns and Ossory The Most Reverend Brendan Comiskey, DD Bishop of Ferns
President	Sir Alfred Beit, Bt
Vice-Presidents	Seán Scallan Sir Claus Moser, KCB, CBE Lt Col David E C Price, MBE
Chairman	Barbara Wallace
Vice-Chairmen	Ted Howlin John O'Connor John Small
Members of Council	Brian Browne, Nicholas Cleary, Turlough Coffey, Don Curtin, Rita Doyle, Ian Fox, Mairéad Furlong, Nicholas Furlong, Jim Golden, Adrian Haythornthwaite, Derek Hill, Prof Anthony Hughes, Derek Joyce, Gerard M Lawlor, Liam Lynch, Tony Lynch, Seamus McCarthy, Cyril Murphy, Marese Murphy, Cyril Nolan, Helen Roche, Eleanor White.

The Festival Committees 1991

Funding and Finance	John O'Connor *(Chairman)*, Turlough Coffey, Ted Howlin, Niall McConnell, John Small, Barbara Wallace
Dublin Committee	Tony Lynch *(Chairman)*, Frank Casey, Brian Coyle, John Daly, John Meagher, Herman O'Brien, Eileen O'Mara Walsh, Eamon Walsh
London Committee	James McCosh *(Chairman)*, Sir David Goodall, Dinah Molloy, Mary V Mullen, Marese Murphy
Repertoire	Ian Fox *(Chairman)*, Sir Alfred Beit Bt, Jane Carty, Nicky Cleary, Gerard Lawlor, Tony Lynch, Miriam O'Connor, Eric Sweeney, Anne Marie Stynes, Derek Walsh
Development	Adrian Haythornthwaite, Niall McConnell, John Small

A history

by Ian Fox

Ian Fox is the music critic of the Sunday Tribune *in Dublin and the Irish correspondent for* Opera. *A well-known broadcaster and lecturer in Ireland, he is a member of the Wexford Festival Council and chairman of its Repertory Committee. He is also a member of the Arts Committee of the Royal Dublin Society. He has wide business interests and is a Fellow of the Institute of Advertising Practitioners in Ireland.*

'A festival of music and joy to refresh the spirits, brighten the sky and flavour the year' is how the London writer and journalist Bernard Levin describes the Wexford Festival, of which he has been a passionate fan since he started his annual pilgrimage in 1967. In his popular book *Conducted Tour*, in which he reviews his twelve favourite festivals, he devotes an entire chapter to Wexford. Thanks to a small band of devoted, largely voluntary enthusiasts, the Festival has grown from modest beginnings to become an important international event. Some day the whole story will be told in detail, but a short history of Wexford Festival Opera still makes fascinating reading.

The kick-off

The original idea for a festival came about during a visit from the great Scottish novelist and founder of the *Gramophone* magazine, Sir Compton Mackenzie, in November 1950, when he addressed the inaugural meeting of the Wexford Opera Study Circle. Dr Tom Walsh, an alert Wexford music lover and chairman of the Circle, knew that the great writer would be in Dublin at the time and persuaded him to take on the extra booking. The meeting was an immense success and the two men struck up a cordial relationship. Sir Compton suggested that rather than talk about opera the Circle should stage its own production. The idea was later bolstered when Dr Walsh picked up a copy of the 1949 Glyndebourne Festival programme during a visit to Foyle's Bookshop in London. On his return home he discussed the proposal with some of his friends, in particular Dr Des Ffrench, another local medical man,

Opposite: Sir Alfred Beit became associated with the Festival in the 1950s; he was chairman of the Festival Council from 1962 to 1966 and has been president of the Festival since 1977.

Eugene McCarthy, owner of White's Hotel, and Seamus O'Dwyer, a postal worker who had an extensive knowledge of opera and was an avid record collector. In May 1951 an attempt was made to raise funds through subscriptions of one guinea each, but it failed to reach the required financial target. However, Dr Walsh decided to go ahead with the project; a 'Festival of Music and the Arts' was planned for October. It is significant that the Festival was born with an inbuilt financial crisis, a problem that in one form or another continues to haunt the Festival Council to this day!

The early years

The Festival launched its first season from 21 October to 4 November, with its centrepiece, a production of Balfe's *The Rose of Castile*, receiving four performances on the first four evenings of November. Right from the start, and in keeping with its original name, the Festival embraced other important artistic activities, including an exhibition of pictures from the National Gallery of Ireland and Ravel's *L'Enfant et les Sortilèges* presented by the Dublin Marionette Group. Recitals were given by the pianist Joseph Weingarten and the violinist Jaroslav Vanacek. The Radio Éireann Light Orchestra, which played for the opera, also provided a concert under the baton of its conductor, Dermot O'Hara.

The Minister for Posts and Telegraphs, Erskine Childers TD, later President of Ireland, addressed the audience on opening night. As the minister responsible for broadcasting, and therefore in charge of the Radio Éireann Light Orchestra, his blessing was essential if the Festival was to continue. His enthusiasm was immediately clear and since then Radio Éireann, later renamed Radio Telefís Éireann, has broadcast every Wexford production, and with one exception has provided the orchestra for the operas. Sir Compton Mackenzie was also present on the opening night and made a typically entertaining speech. He himself later became Festival president, a position he maintained for the remaining twenty-one years of his life. With this kind of support and enthusiastic audiences, the organisers realised they had a considerable success on their hands. They formalised a working Council and set about planning a second year, selecting a more ambitious work with their new-found confidence.

It is hard now to think of Donizetti's charming *L'Elisir d'Amore* as a musical rarity, but it wasn't well known at that time. Caruso had appeared in it many times, and Schipa and Gigli were fond of its melodious phrases, but since the war it was seldom performed outside its native Italy. However, it had been successfully revived at Covent Garden in 1950 with the young Tito Gobbi in the cast, and it was with some audacity that Festival chairman Dr Walsh decided

to present it on the tiny Theatre Royal stage. The building was minuscule and the conditions wretched for the singers, who had to dress for their roles in their hotel rooms and arrive at the theatre in costume and make-up. But Dr Walsh set his sights high and revealed his talent for attracting important artists. He engaged Peter Ebert, the brilliant son of the great Glyndebourne producer Carl Ebert, to direct the production. He also brought in four important international singers, in particular Nicola Monti, the young Italian tenor who was being hailed as the successor to Tito Schipa. Monti made a huge impression on the audiences, professionally and personally, and returned for four further seasons: *Don Pasquale* (1953), *La Sonnambula* (1954), *La Cenerentola* (1956) and, later, *L'Amico Fritz* (1962). A happy, easy-going atmosphere developed in these early years, with Monti and the other soloists singing songs and arias late into the night in the town's hotels and bars.

It was with the 1955 season that the Festival's real reputation for unearthing neglected operas commenced. It was also the beginning of the two-opera seasons, later broadened to three productions per Festival in 1963. For this larger undertaking, Dr Walsh chose Puccini's *Manon Lescaut* and the lesser known *Der Wildschütz* by Albert Lortzing. From then on the Festival moved steadily into a pattern of presenting the more rarified sections of the operatic repertory, and eventually it became the progenitor

of such important revivals as the works of Rossini, Massenet, the Ricci brothers and many others. The list of talented young singers which Dr Walsh contracted is today quite mouth-watering: Heather Harper, April Cantelo, Graziella Sciutti, Geraint Evans, Paolo Montarsolo, Fiorenza Cossotto, Plinio Clabassi and Janet Baker are some of the principals who appeared at the Festival during its formative first decade.

The very success of the Festival was creating increasing problems for those trying to cope with the primitive backstage conditions in the theatre. Sir Alfred Beit, a former Conservative MP and person of great influence, became involved with the Festival in the late 1950s. Sir Alfred had bought and restored Russborough House in County Wicklow, one of the country's finest Georgian mansions, in 1952, to which he brought his family's remarkable art collection. Plans to build a new opera house to replace the unsuitable Theatre Royal had been in the air for some time, but the cost, estimated at £50,000, was too high. Instead, a reconstruction appeal was launched and Sir Alfred persuaded the Gulbenkian Foundation to provide £15,000 as the major part of the required funding. The scale of the work prevented the Festival taking place in 1960, but the much improved theatre was ready for the 1961 season. Dr Walsh had a difference of opinion with Radio Éireann over whether the Light Orchestra or the Symphony should

Wilfred Judd, who first came to the Festival as stage manager, produced the 1980 presentation of Handel's Orlando, *conducted by his brother James Judd. Since then he has established an important international career in the world's leading opera houses.*

The distinguished baritone Benjamin Luxon performed the two great Schubert song cycles Die Schöne Müllerin *and* Winterreise *in the Theatre Royal during the 1978 Festival.*

Far left:
The Wexford Festival Singers have been a central feature of the Festival for many years. Their repertory has ranged from Rossini's 'Petite messe Solonnelle' in their first year, 1974, to Handel's 'L'Allegro, il Penseroso ed il Moderato' in 1990. Having started in the Friary church, the choir settled in Rowe Street church, where this photograph was taken.

Brian Dickie was artistic director from 1967 to 1973. Today he is general administrator at Glyndebourne.

Today David Fielding is one of the world's most sought after designers. He has had a close association with the Festival for many years, beginning with Mayr's Medea in Corinto *in 1974. His staging of Britten's* The Turn of the Screw *(1976), with producer Adrian Slack, has long been regarded as a* tour de force. *In 1988 he became the first and only person both to produce and design the same opera, Mercadante's* Elisa e Claudio.

be made available for the Festival. He decided to experiment with the Liverpool Philharmonic, a decision which did not prove a great success. Fortunately the problems were sorted out and the Radio Éireann Symphony started its long and continuing reign at Wexford in 1962. Since then it has undergone two name changes: to the Radio Telefís Éireann Symphony, following the creation of the Radio Telefís Authority to deal with the new national television service, and to the National Symphony Orchestra of Ireland in 1990. Apart from the use of a special baroque ensemble to play for Cavalli's 1652 opera *Eritrea* (1975) and the two-piano accompaniment used in Balfe's *The Siege of Rochelle* (1963), the orchestra has played for every performance since, giving sterling service for thirty years across an amazingly diverse range of musical styles.

The 1961 season wasn't a great success, but 1962 saw a full return to form, particularly with the appearance of a brilliant young soprano from Modena, Mirella Freni, in *I Puritani*, and a delightful *L'Amico Fritz* with a strong cast which included two major Irish artists, Veronica Dunne and Bernadette Greevy, in the company of the still splendid Nicola Monti. In 1963 the season was extended to three operas, and in the confident atmosphere of the 1960s a number of Wexford's most memorable productions were staged, including Massenet's *Don Quichotte* (1965) which introduced the conductor Albert Rosen to Ireland; he was later to become principal conductor of the RTE Symphony and has directed a number of great Festival presentations.

Parallel developments

As it progressed the Festival did not neglect is wider artistic ambitions, and a number of other important annual events were launched. The Festival Forum began in 1952 under the chairmanship of the entertaining Wexford solicitor, Fintan O'Connor. Originally intended as a filler for Saturday nights, when there was no opera performance, the Forum became a long-lived part of the Festival's associated activities, continuing until the early 1970s. The first panel comprised the *Irish Times* cookery writer Mary Frances Keating; the leader of the political party Clan na Poblachta and later Nobel Peace Prize winner, Seán McBride SC; Erskine Childers TD, and the ebullient barrister and genealogist Eoin 'The Pope' O'Mahony, who chaired his own Radio Éireann programme *Meet the Clans* for many years. The Dublin University Players paid their first annual

Michael Geliot was for many years resident producer with the Welsh National Opera; his Wexford productions included Albert Herring *(Britten, 1970) and* Il Pirata *(Bellini, 1972).*

Jane Glover was the only woman to conduct at Wexford, making her debut with Cavalli's Eritrea *in 1975 and returning for Gluck's* Orfeo ed Euridice *in 1977.*

visit to the Festival in 1955, and each year the Festival ran an extensive film programme, at a time when operatic films or important foreign movies were considered too 'arty' for general release in Ireland. Festival tours were organised by Dr George Haddon, and in more recent years by Nicholas Furlong, which provided visitors with the opportunity to learn something of the rich history of the town and county. Another distinguished cabaret visitor was the great musical comedienne, Anna Russell, whose 1958 appearance at Wexford preceded her only Dublin performance by a number of years.

Changes in directorship and approach

In December 1966 Sir Alfred Beit, who had become Festival chairman, made the surprise announcement that Dr Walsh had decided to retire, and the next season would be his last as artistic director. There are many versions of how this decision came about. Certainly relationships between Dr Walsh and the Festival Council had become increasingly strained. He had been uneasy about the decision to stage Verdi's popular *La Traviata* in 1965, and he questioned the direction the Festival was taking. In an interview in *Opera* magazine he stated: 'Whatever reason the Council now had for running the Festival, it was no longer for the advancement of opera in Ireland. So, since no further development of opera was intended, I decided to resign.' There were those who wondered from where this policy of operatic advancement had emerged and how Dr Walsh could distance himself from the programming which he himself created and largely chose. One might place such an accusation at the feet of successive governments and Arts Councils in Ireland, but not at the ever-progressive Wexford Festival. His withdrawal was absolute, and the decision to appoint a professional director was undertaken, though where the £2,000 a year for such a salary would be found no one knew.

The position was advertised and a most unlikely applicant emerged. Walter Legge was living in semi-retirement in Switzerland. He was a legendary figure in the music world: the leading record producer of his era, the founder of the Philharmonia Orchestra and husband of the beautiful Elizabeth Schwarzkopf. His interest in undertaking the post was a considerable imprimatur on the fame of the Festival and his appointment was greeted with delight. It was short-

Aroldo. Act 1, Scene 2. Design by Micheál MacLiammóir.

Many ensembles have appeared in the Festival's extensive associated concerts and recitals. The Hesketh Piano Trio from Dublin comprised Therese Timoney, Gillian Smith and Betty Sullivan and played an all-Schubert programme at the 1978 Festival.

lived; Legge had a heart attack in January 1967 and had to withdraw even before he had visited Wexford.

A new search commenced and a young Glyndebourne executive, 26-year-old Brian Dickie, was chosen as the

Left: *Dennis O'Neill was a regular visitor to the Festival, moving from comprimario to leading roles in the 1970s. Today he is one of the most sought-after tenors in the world.*

Right: *The 1980 production of* Of Mice and Men *was attended by the opera's composer, Carlisle Floyd. He is seen, third from the left, with Festival administrator David Collopy, chairman Jim Golden and Dr Maeve Hillery, wife of the President of Ireland, who is a notable supporter of the Festival.*

Festival's first professional director. He had recently been appointed administrator of the Glyndebourne Touring Opera. He had Irish family connections as well as having studied at Trinity College Dublin. Despite his youth he had been with Glyndebourne for five years and he immediately displayed a talent for organisation and a deep understanding of the needs of opera. He could be ascerbic on occasions, and his annual tourneys with the media at the Festival press conferences produced some memorable exchanges. But he proved to have one essential ability: a knack for matching the right voices to the operas he chose. A new era of outstanding singing emerged in Wexford, quite different to that of the past but every bit as rewarding. He also took a fresh look at the repertory. More French music was heard, and Russian and Czech opera was introduced. Meanwhile, Dr Walsh began a whole new career as an opera historian. He had already produced a small volume on *Opera in Old Dublin*, published by the Festival in 1952, but now he undertook much larger projects, including a study of Second Empire opera in France, opera in Dublin from 1705 to 1797, and a history of the Monte Carlo Opera Company.

Dickie decided to maintain the pattern of three productions per year, a format which was to continue to the present day. Festival president Sir Compton Mackenzie died in 1972 and was succeeded by the American philanthropist and opera lover, Lauder Greenway. Dickie later succeeded Moran Caplat as general administrator at Glyndebourne, but pressure of work became too great and 1973 was his last season at Wexford. He could look back on seven highly successful years, which had proved that modern opera was box-office at Wexford. There were many memorable

productions, such as Janáček's *Katá Kavanová* (1972), with Sona Cervena's brilliant interpretation of the mother, and Prokofiev's *The Gambler*, spectacularly produced by David Pountney. In 1972 two Wexford productions, *Katá Kabanová* and *Il Pirata*, were transported to the York Festival, where they met with considerable success. Dickie introduced the splendid Martinique soprano Christiane Eda-Pierre to Wexford audiences, with *Lakmé* (1970), *Les Pêcheurs de Perles* (1971), and *Il Pirata* (1972). He also brought such important names as Jill Gomez, Alexander Oliver, Norma Burrowes, Matti Salminen and Dennis O'Neill. He introduced a Glyndebourne production style, employing many producers and designers who today are among the world's most sought-after experts. These included producers David Pountney, John Cox and Patrick Libby, and designers John Stoddart, John Fraser, Bernard Culshaw, Roger Butlin and Adam Pollock. His musical directors include names like David Lloyd-Jones, David Atherton, Guy Barbier, Kenneth Montgomery and Albert Rosen.

Dickie's successor was the amiable Scot, Thomson Smillie, from Glasgow. He had been publicity officer at Scottish Opera but soon displayed an exciting talent which brought new successes and subtle changes to the Festival. He was the first to crystallise the annual selection of repertory into one main 'singers' opera, one comedy and one 'thinking piece'. While it has not been possible to observe this formula exactly, Smillie and his successors have maintained an attitude which fits in broadly with this approach. He began his term in 1974 in a season which included Massenet's *Thaïs*. This French composer's music had been in

Left: *Designer Douglas Heap created the settings for Puccini's* Edgar *in 1980, with costumes by Jane Law. Earlier he had designed Montemezzi's* L'Amore dei Tre Re *(1979).*

Right: *Thomson Smillie served as artistic director from 1974 to 1978. He is seen here in 1975 (right) with the general administrator Andrew Potter and his delightful assistant Sally Thomas, who even played a mime role in one production.*

considerable eclipse for over fifty years, although Dr Walsh had spotted his potential in the memorable 1965 production of *Don Quichotte* starring Miroslav Cangalovic. Following the Wexford revival, opera companies began to re-examine *Thaïs*, and a batch of new productions appeared, particularly in the USA. The reassessment of Massenet has continued at Wexford, with a total of six revivals to date. French music owes much to the Festival as, apart from Massenet, the neglected works of Auber, Bizet, Boïeldieu, Delibes, Gounod, Lalo and Thomas have all received outstanding presentations.

The year 1976 was the silver jubilee of the Festival. Wexford Corporation paid tribute to Dr Walsh by conferring the Freedom of the Borough on him. It was also Lauder Greenway's last season as Festival president; he retired through ill health and was succeeded by Sir Alfred Beit, a former Festival chairman and Council member since 1959. The season also saw one of the Festival's most remarkable performances: Benjamin Britten's *The Turn of the Screw* in an astonishingly fluid production by Adrian Slack, with designs by David Fielding. Albert Rosen conducted this memorable presentation, whose cast included Jane Manning, Dublin soprano Ann Cant, and an amazing 14-year-old local bog soprano, James McGuire, as Myles.

In 1977 Smillie persuaded one of the greatest figures of Italian opera, Sesto Bruscantini, to make his first visit to the Festival. He starred in a remarkable triple bill which included a brilliant one-man performance in Cimarosa's *Il Maestro di Capella*, leading roles in Pergoelsi's *La Serva Padrona*, and a one-act comedy by the long forgotten Ricci brothers, *La Serva e l'Ussero* (1836). The success of this

led to a full-length Ricci opera in 1979, *Crispino e la Comare*, again with Bruscantini both singing the buffo role of Crispino and directing the whole delightful production. A number of important names were associated with this presentation: soprano Lucia Aliberti, buffo Gianni Socci and Dublin mezzo Ruth Maher, who all received considerable acclaim. The conductor was James Judd and the designer Tim Reed; once again Wexford audiences were meeting the great names of the era as well as some of the most exciting emerging talent. The revival of a Ricci brothers' opera was in itself another feather in Wexford's exploratory cap.

In 1978 Smillie used his close association with Scottish Opera to organise a joint production, and Smetana's charming lyric comedy *The Two Widows* was first staged at Wexford and later performed by the Glasgow company on its tours. It was to bring Smillie's period at the Festival to a highly satisfactory conclusion. He had been spotted by American interests and was offered the post of general manager with Sarah Cauldwell's famous Boston Opera Company. Later he moved to Kentucky Opera, where he is now chief executive. In his five seasons Smillie successfully developed and refined the direction established by Dickie. His choice was eclectic: he brought the only full-scale baroque production to the Festival (Cavalli's *Eritrea*, 1975), through which Dublin-born mezzo Ann Murray met her husband, tenor Philip Landgridge; he brought the inestimable Bruscantini to Wexford and introduced operas by Nicolai (*The Merry Wives of Windsor*) and d'Albert (*Tiefland*). Overall, he expanded the programme for recitals and associated events so that a visit to the Festival became an increasingly busy affair.

21

In 1979 Adrian Slack became artistic director. As a producer he was the first practitioner to hold the post and was best known through his marvellous production *The Turn of the Screw*, one of the four operas he had staged at Wexford. His stay was short, just three seasons, but he maintained a high quality in his nine presentations. Carlisle Floyd's *Of Mice and Men*, the first opera by a living composer, was part of his 1980 season. His term also saw the aforementioned *Crispino e la Comare*, and he staged *Zaïde*, the first Mozart opera since 1971, which was also taken to the Grand Opera House, Belfast, as part of the 1981 Festival at Queen's.

In 1982 Elaine Padmore emerged as the Festival's first lady at the helm. As the producer with BBC's Radio Three, she had been responsible for many broadcasts of Wexford operas in the United Kingdom. She was also involved in the selection of operas for broadcasting and therefore was a regular listener to unusual works recorded around the world. She is the first professional musician to hold the post

Bottom: *Festival map of Wexford, 1958.*

Top, opposite: *An exhibition of Early, Renaissance and Late Italian paintings from the National Gallery of Ireland was a feature of the 1975 Festival.*

Bottom, opposite: Left to right *Mr Thomson Smillie, artistic director, Wexford Festival; Mr Seán Scallan, chairman, Wexford Festival; Cllr. Avril Doyle, Mayor of Wexford; Mr William Murphy, chairman, Southeast Tourism; Mr Nicholas Furlong, PRO Wexford Festival, admiring a special wall-hanging presented by Southeast Tourism to each guest at the press dinner in Johnstown Castle.*

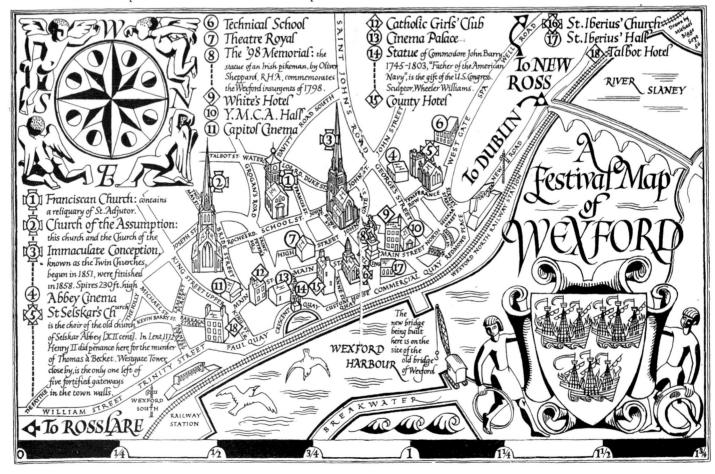

Patrick Libby made his Wexford debut in 1970 as producer of the double bill L'Inganno Felice *(Rossini) and* Giovedi Grasso *(Donizetti), and showed a fine touch for high comedy; he returned for* L'Ajo nell'Imbarazzo *(Donizetti, 1973) and* The Merry Wives of Windsor *(Nicolai, 1976), by which time he was working at Glyndebourne, Covent Garden and the Metropolitan, New York.*

Albert Rosen photographed at the time he made his Irish debut conducting the memorable 1965 production of Massenet's Don Quichotte. *Later he settled in Ireland and became chief conductor of the Radio Telefís Éireann Symphony Orchestra (now the National Symphony Orchestra). He has been a frequent visitor to the Festival, with a record fifteen operas to his credit.*

Stewart Trotter staged the memorable production of Of Mice and Men *(1980). Before that he had been responsible for the 1979 production of Montemezzi's* L'Amore dei Tre Re *(1979).*

of artistic director and her ten years at Wexford have been highly successful. Like Brian Dickie, she has a remarkable ability for spotting talent and has brought a whole new generation of exciting young singers to the Festival. In her work with the Festival's Repertory Committee, which oversees the selection of operas for production, she displays her broad musical tastes, which are reflected in the impressive range of opera that has been covered. In thirty productions, including 1991, there are works by such neglected Italian composers as Alfano, Wolf-Ferrari, Cimarosa, Catalani, Mercadante, Busoni, Gazzaniga and Giordano; she has brought Marschner back to public attention in two highly controversial productions in 1983 and 1989; under her direction another living composer, Nicholas Maw, has joined the ranks, and an eclectic selection of international names has appeared, including Weill, Humperdinck and Thomas. The choice of production teams and singers has been equally successful, even allowing for the fact that many of the younger stars have yet to make it to the top in the international operatic world and may be relatively unknown at present. A few examples will demonstrate the range: conductors Robin Stapleton, Arnold Oestman, Jan Latham-Koenig and Marco Guidarini; producers Nicholas Hytner, Michael McCaffrey, Patrick Mason and Jean Claude Auvray; designers Joe Vaněk, Russell Craig, Richard Aylwin and Ruari Murchinson; and singers Sergei Leiferkus, Raul Giminez, Patrick Power, Cynthia Clarey, Kathleen Kuhlmann, Alessandra Marc, Cyndia Sieden and Karen Notare.

Ongoing success

Many significant changes have occurred during this last decade, in co-operation with two dynamic and far-seeing Festival chairmen, Jim Golden and Barbara Wallace. In particular, the Opera Scenes project has been developed into one of the core events, playing two different programmes to packed houses every year. They are seen as a means of bringing some opera to the Festival at a low ticket price. This has enabled the artistic director to offer more work to young singers, thus encouraging them to come to Wexford in spite of the modest financial reward. A number of productions have visited the Queen Elizabeth Hall in London, starting in 1986 with *Tancredi*, thereby broadening the international interest in Wexford, and in

Adrian Slack first came to Wexford to direct Medea in Corinto *(1974) and later staged* La Pietra del Paragone *(1975) and the remarkable* The Turn of the Screw *(1976). He served as artistic director from 1979 to 1981.*

The Czech designer John Cervenka devised the settings for Carlisle Floyd's opera Of Mice and Men *in 1980.*

Julian Hope first came to Wexford to stage the 1977 production of Massenet's Hérodiade, *returning for Spontini's* La Vestale *(1979) and Donizetti's* Linda di Chamounix *(1983).*

Tim Reed's early career was closely associated with Wexford. Originally a member of the stage crew he leaped to fame with his imaginative sets for Crispino e la Comare *(1979). He also designed the triple bill the previous year and has returned for* Un Giorno di Regno *(1981),* La Vedova Scaltra *(1983), and* Cendrillon *(1987).*

1988 the three Festival presentations were recorded on videotape and have been shown around the world.

The sustained success of the Festival for forty years has not been achieved without considerable hard work. A Development Committee was formed in the late 1970s and reported to the Council in 1980. Following its recommendations, much has been accomplished. Considerable rebuilding and re-equipping of the Theatre Royal has been undertaken, culminating in the major restyling of the tiny auditorium in 1988 so as to increase accommodation to 550 seats. The same year Jerome Hynes was appointed as the first full-time managing director, and in 1989 he increased the Festival's duration by six days, adding one extra performance of each opera as well as three nights of recitals. In 1991 the Festival moves to a continuous eighteen-night schedule, with six performances of each opera. In May 1990 the Festival ran its first 'Spring School', with lectures on opera and the problems it faces today, presented by a team of expert speakers headed by Andrew Porter of the *New Yorker*. This venture was repeated in 1991 when Rodney Milnes of *Opera* magazine was the featured guest, and the weekend tied in with the production of *The Rose of Castile* which was staged with professional singers and a young production team as part

Limerick-born tenor Francis Egerton made his Festival debut in the memorable 1965 production of Mozart's La Finta Giardiniera *and has returned to Wexford on many occasions, most recently as Brother Timothy in Maw's* The Rising of the Moon *(1990).*

Simon Joly first came to Wexford as chorus master in 1981 and later conducted The Rise and Fall of the City of Mahagonny *(1985), the double bill in 1988 and* The Rising of the Moon *(1990).*

of a special week-long training session for students wishing to gain experience in backstage crafts. The Festival is deeply concerned about educational opportunities for students in the field of opera and drama.

Space does not permit a review of all the associated events which have played an important part in creating the rich tapestry of activities surrounding the opera productions. The Opera Scenes now draws packed houses; the Wexford Festival Singers present an annual concert; a range of recitals and cabaret performances are given throughout each Festival, and the Arts Centre stages exhibitions, poetry readings and plays. Many of these activities were originally developed by the Festival Council, but were passed on to independent organisers as they grew in size; in this way the Festival has provided the starting point for most of the extensive arts activities centred in Wexford today. A complete sub-culture of non-associated exhibitions, theatrical shows, sporting events and other activities has been drawn to Wexford during Festival time, helping to create a truly festive atmosphere.

Funding for the Festival

Ask any member of Council what takes up most time at Council meetings and the reply will be 'money'. There is a running joke that when the Repertory Committee presents its annual report to Council, with its recommendations for the following season, that this is the only time the agenda permits any discussion of the core product — the operas. While this is not literally true, of course, it illustrates the central role that funding takes in any artistic venture. In 1989 a study was commissioned from John O'Hagan, the Professor of Economics at Trinity College Dublin, in which he examined the economic and social contribution of Wexford to the local environment and the country as a whole. He showed that the Festival is decidedly underfunded by the state, which contributes only 28 per cent of the overall cost, compared to the UK experience, where the Welsh National Opera receives 70 per cent of its finance from the Arts Council and local government, and Opera North as much as 78 per cent. The situation across the European Community reveals an even greater level of state support. This means that the Wexford Festival has to rely much more on commercial sponsorship than its European counterparts. The situation is different in the United States, where corporate sponsorship is common practice. The lack of state funding here is ill-deserved, given the Festival's tremendous impact on tourism and the splendid public relations job it does for the image of Ireland abroad. Professor O'Hagan stresses the importance of such a Festival in influencing the establishment of businesses in the country, and quotes a UK survey which suggests that 'a strong cultural infrastructure is a business asset for a region'. The Festival owes an enormous debt of gratitude to its principal sponsors, in particular Guinness and Radio Telefís Éireann.

Whether the argument is tourism, business development or sheer artistic merit, the Wexford Festival seems to give a lot more than it receives in return from state coffers. The acid test, however, is how well it succeeds with its key function, and Edward Greenfield, the distinguished music critic and broadcaster, summed it up when he wrote: 'For nearly forty years the Wexford Festival has been finding buried operatic treasure to put the grandest metropolitan opera houses to shame.' Despite all the ups and downs the Festival has experienced, with changes of personnel, financial dramas or technical problems, the spirit of Wexford appears to be as clear and firm as it always has been. This can only be because the people of Wexford, who provide the bulk of voluntary workers, want the Festival to happen. So long as their determination remains, and it seems as alive as ever forty years on, then the Festival, too, will move from triumph to triumph.

The thrill of the new

by Elaine Padmore

Elaine Padmore *looks back over nearly twenty years of Wexford visits and chooses some of the highlights of her ten years as artistic director.*

It began for me in 1973, when I walked through the doors of the Theatre Royal for the first time. I was a young BBC producer standing in for the head of opera, Julian Budden, who'd gone off to Italy to research his first great Verdi book.

I was to look after the BBC's live relay of Prokofiev's *The Gambler*. It was before the improvements had been made to the front of the house and the audience used to run down the street to the Tower bar for interval drinks: getting them back again was a problem. Seán Scallan, the concerned and courteous chairman, was determined that the performance should be punctual for the BBC. It was the one occasion in my experience when anyone promised to ring bells in hotels and bars to get the show on the air at the promised time.

It was my first visit to Ireland and it was not love at first sight. I stayed some miles outside of town, in a farmhouse buzzing with flies, and had difficulties negotiating the cowpats in the yard at night, in the pitch dark, wearing long skirts and high heels. But the farmer's wife threw her arms round me when we parted, with a 'Sure to God I hope we'll meet again' – an expression I hadn't heard before – and I knew I could care a lot for people who said such things.

It was three years on, 1976, before my next visit, and now I was head of opera at the BBC. For the following six years the BBC paid me to spend at least a week at the Festival, taking care of the broadcasts. Few in the audience knew the risks and perils of those broadcasts, which used to be conducted from a tin shack up a ladder on the roof, until the roof was removed and the shack along with it. Nowadays there's a backstage room for the convenience of broadcasters, but the complexities of transmitting from the Theatre Royal to the British Isles are still great. It's easier to beam home the sound of the BBC Symphony Orchestra on tour in Tokyo than to guarantee safe passage to the sound leaving the Theatre Royal via lines to Belfast, transmitters prone to icing up even in October, GPO lines and switching centres carrying the sound across to Manchester, then to Birmingham and hence to London. The technical hitches on air were numerous: as recently as 1989 the broadcast of *Der Templer und die Jüdin* broke down halfway through and had to be abandoned. No wonder the team in the tin shack drew together in adversity. I remember the companionship of one of my first Irish friends, the irrepressible RTE balancer Eamonn Timoney, who shook with nerves on a BBC broadcast night and made up for it afterwards by celebrating till dawn. Then there was the famous Radio Three announcer Tom Crowe, who came over to present the broadcasts and was one year heard live on air at 8.30 whispering 'Have we started yet Elaine?'

There was also the nearest I ever came to a punch-up with a producer (he the worse for drink) who, overhearing my quite harmless enquiry to the artistic director about the duration of intervals in his opera, hurled abuse at me in White's Hotel for a good ten minutes on the grounds that I was one of those useless bureaucrats who cared more about the length of the intervals than the quality of the performance.

Those BBC years hold memories of friendships renewed from year to year. There was the stern man in the box office, Jim Golden, who after a year or two smiled at me when handing over my tickets (and much later, as chairman, offered me the job of artistic director). The pleasure of returning to favourite haunts, to people in shops, homes, hotels, bars. The late-lamented Feena Kelly at the Crown Bar, where opera singers unwound — and sang — late into the night. That first Irish coffee of the year; it doesn't taste the same in England, any more than they say the Guinness does. The glittering extravagance of those splendid Guinness buffets to which invitations were prized trophies. The fascination of Irish conversation with its easy flow, brilliantly turned phrases and outrageous humour. The pleasure — rare for a big city dweller — of being recognised in a small town from one year to the next. Do Tommy in the Talbot Hotel diningroom and Michael in White's Bar know that their knack of remembering and welcoming visitors has fixed them as high on the list of faces eagerly sought out as the much-loved owners, the Lynches and the Smalls?

I remember the pleasure of discovering coastline and castles, villages and bird sanctuaries: the late night drives down to Carne and other gastronomic havens, cruising lunch trips on *The Galley* from New Ross, walks on the beach at Rosslare, with sunsets to defy all lighting designers. I'm glad I had the chance to get to know the coast and the county in those annual visits, because since 1982 I've never again had the time for outings. At least I have a bit of knowledge to pass on to enquiring Festival-goers eager for a day's drive, and have some sense of the delights *outside* the Theatre Royal that make up the total experience of a visit to Wexford.

It never crossed my mind in those years that I would be invited to direct the Festival. When I was, and said yes, it changed my life. A decade on, the memories are sharply focussed on the stage of the Theatre Royal, a rich crop harvested from every Festival: visual memories, vocal memories, ghastly memories, proud memories.

Visual memories

The visual memories begin with the cool green beauty of David Fielding's elegant mirrored set for *Sakùntala*. The film of a British-raj-in-India elephant hunt shown in the same opera in lieu of a ballet (for which there wasn't space), the film's period feel unexpectedly enhanced on first night by the sepia coloration that enclosed the final frames — as the projector gently incinerated it. John Otto's exquisite painted set for *L'Isola Disabitata*, with shutters that opened very slowly to reveal the brilliance of sea and jungle behind. The hand-painted decoration on Tim Reed's costumes for *La Vedova Scaltra*. The exquisite detail of the black and white backdrop painted for *Linda di Chamounix* by Chris Clark. More ravishing costumes in Peter J Davison's design for *Mitridate*. The way the black and white tartan world of *La Dame Blanche* gradually took on more colour until the final *coup de théâtre* as the technicolour dream castle was unfurled. A set of stunning effectiveness by Ruari Murchison for *Zazà*, with its applause-drawing moment when the hero stood at the window of his apartment and we suddenly recognised that the portrait hanging in Zazà's room was of him in that very position.

The brilliant theatricality of the Richard Jones/Richard Hudson *Mignon* with its realistic fire, stage curtains crashing down and actors running through the audience. The outstanding professionalism of the American team of Francesca Zambello and Neil Peter Jampolis who created a magical *Devil and Kate,* later seen at the Opera Theatre of St Louis. The three productions of the Patrick Mason/Joe Vaněk team, beginning with the sensational success of *La cena delle beffe* — an opera first suggested to me by a good friend, the late Freddy Caracciolo, who was on the Wexford Repertoire Committee and who had known Giordano in Italy. Then the double bill of *Don Giovanni* and *Turandot*; and culminating in Prokofiev's *The Duenna,* one of the most dazzling productions I've seen at Wexford, in the most inventive set.

The startling expressionistic intensity of the Stephen Pimlott/David Fielding *Hans Heiling*, with Heiling, torn between human and fairy worlds, finally revealed as a schizophrenic in a mental institution. Well, how *do* you produce an opera in the late twentieth century about a man who thinks he's king of the fairies? I'm glad there was a degree of controversy: I would not wish Wexford to become a museum of comfort culture from which confrontation and provocation were totally excluded. I treasure the (anonymous) postcard of an Irish donkey sent to me with the message 'this donkey could have done a better production of *Hans Heiling* than we saw in Wexford'.

The productions of *Mahagonny* and *Der Templer und die Jüdin* have also touched nerves of reaction, though in general Wexford repertoire is unfamiliar enough to have the thrill of the new about it without the same need for reinterpretation as comes with over-frequent repetitions of the same popular operas.

Horror memories

Horror memories (just a couple will do): sitting in the theatre on the first night of *Le Jongleur de Notre Dame* as Patrick Power in the huge title role gradually lost his voice during the course of Act One (it was also a live broadcast). The year Sealink chose October to go on strike (in 1986), leaving a substantial amount of our sets and lights on the wrong side of the Irish Sea.

Musical thrills

For me the greatest thrills are the musical ones, the delight in discovering new voices and the moment of hearing them in combination for the first time. It's good to discover that the soprano from Sweden and the tenor from Czechoslovakia blend as well as you thought they would! Certain musical moments stand out: the secret pleasure of knowing that however overwhelmed the audience at *La cena delle beffe* might be by the voices of Miriam Gauci, Fabio Armiliato and Luis Giron May in Act One, Act Two would bring the glorious soaring tones of Alessandra Marc, a voice of unrivalled power and beauty in my Wexford years. The immaculate duetting of Kathleen Kuhlmann and Inga Nielsen in *Tancredi* and of Lena Nordin and Cyndia Sieden in *Mitridate*. The musicianship of Neil Jenkins singing complicated rhythms while playing the musical glasses at the end of *The Duenna*. The radiant singing of Daniela Bechly as the goosegirl in *Königskinder*. She came to audition for me in Düsseldorf; as did Bruce Ford, whose unfailing top Ds were one of the musical thrills of *Tancredi*. It was the first Wexford production to go to London's South Bank, followed by *La Straniera*, *Elisa e Claudio* and *Mitridate* in annual succession. (Our extended Festival period has temporarily halted the visits, soon to be resumed).

The distinctive burnished mezzo of Cynthia Clarey, a great audience favourite who first sang a villain in Handel's *Ariodante*, returned in the title role of *Mignon* and then as the jilted bride in *La Straniera*, along with her equally popular husband, baritone Jake Gardner. The pleasure of

hearing Norman Bailey on the Wexford stage for the first time, albeit late in his career, bringing such unexpected humour to the role of the Commendatore in Gazzaniga's *Don Giovanni* that we invented the new voice category of Helden-Buffo for him. And the delight of getting Francis Egerton back to Wexford after years of unsuccessful attempts, in the role of Brother Timothy in Nicholas Maw's opera *The Rising of the Moon* — which though actually written for him he did not sing at the Glyndebourne première in 1970.

Not all auditions are conventional, and for every singer who's been recruited after performances or personal audition, there's another first heard on tape or disc. An unknown Argentine tenor named Raul Gimenez was suggested to me by an agent (who hadn't actually heard him, just *of* him) when I was looking for a suitable coloratura tenor for Cimarosa's *Le Astuzie Femminili*. I tracked him down, dispatched to him a blank cassette and the music for a couple of arias from the opera, and asked him to learn and record them for me as quickly as possible. Back from Buenos Aires came the tape with Raul's lovely musical tones clearly in evidence. He returned to Wexford a second time for *Ariodante* before increasing fame took him away. That's the usual pattern with the outstanding 'finds' — after one or two Festival appearances they hit the big league and are lost to us.

We were luckier with Sergei Leiferkus. I heard him on an obscure Russian record of singers from Leningrad's Kirov Opera and though I was extremely nervous about hiring a Russian at a time (before Glasnost) when sudden cancellations were commonplace, there was something compelling about that voice…so I engaged him to sing in *Grisélidis*. He missed connecting flights and as I waited for him to arrive for hours in White's Hotel (usual greeting place for arriving artists) I feared the worst. Then in walked this man in a furry Russian hat. He spoke no English but he knew who I was and we gave each other a big hug. It was quite a moment for him too. Wexford was alive with excitement the next day when he sang his first rehearsal. After that first sensational year he came back three times. *Hans Heiling* was chosen as a vehicle for him; then he appeared as the genial monk Boniface in *Le Jongleur de Notre Dame* and as the mysterious fiddler in *Königskinder*. By that time he was much in demand internationally and his Wexford years were inevitably at an end. His concert at the fortieth Festival marks the tenth anniversary of his first appearance.

Memories, too, of the impassioned playing drawn from the National Symphony Orchestra by Albert Rosen in many a large-scale score, carefully tailored by him to fit the '45 only' limitation on bodies in the pit. The Gallic charm of another Wexford favourite, conductor Yan Pascal Tortelier, whose violin recital, presented in elegant fractured English, will long be remembered.

Some Wexford pleasures repeat themselves endlessly. The first sniff of the autumn air perfumed with peat smoke; the sharp outline of the twin church spires in a well-lit dusk, the shop windows being dressed to compete in the Festival competition; the strings of light bulbs going up along High Street (how can so inconspicuous a backstreet be called that?) brightening the way to its most prestigious front door. I feel as proud of those strings of bulbs as if they were seven miles of Blackpool Illuminations, and always feel a twinge of disappointment if they've been switched off by the time I leave the theatre.

THE EARLY DAYS

'First lady of song'

Happy recollections *by Nellie Walsh*

As the innkeeper in The Rose of Castile, **Nellie Walsh**, *sister of the Festival's founding director, was the first voice ever to be heard in a Festival production. Happily she is still a member of the chorus. Here she records some of her memories and highlights of forty years singing at Wexford.*

Sir Compton Mackenzie speaking from the stage of the Theatre Royal after the first night of the 1951 Festival. Behind him are James Cuthbert, Murray Dickie, Dermot O'Hara, Maureen Springer, Dr Tom Walsh, Angela O'Connor, James Browne, Statia Keys, Nellie Walsh and the then Minister for Posts and Telegraphs, Erskine Childers, who was later President of Ireland.

In 1951, when the Wexford Festival launched its first season, it was Radio Éireann who decided if the persons put forward by the Festival Council for minor parts were of an 'acceptable standard'. I had undertaken a lot of concert work and broadcasts, so I was given their approval. As a result I had the privilege of being the first soloist ever to be heard in Wexford Festival Opera.

The Rose of Castile was chosen as our first production because its composer Michael Balfe had once lived in Wexford, where his father was a band-master. Also because it was one of Balfe's lesser-known works – in keeping with the Festival's policy of staging rare and forgotten operas. There was actually a reward of £5 offered to anyone who could establish and prove the house where the Balfe family had lived; the money was never claimed, although there was many an effort to win it. Nevertheless, the search certainly added to the excitement of the first performance

of the Wexford Festival Opera, and it was a great success. But when it came to the second year, all hands were again needed on deck. A once-off production is one thing, but an established annual Festival implied better performances, better operas, better standards each season. The Council's policy was to produce operas seldom performed, works which through no fault of the writer or composer just hadn't clicked, or had suffered because there were a lot of other works to choose from at the time. Many little-known compositions have had the dust shaken off them during a Wexford Festival, and subsequently were produced in larger opera houses.

One of our main boasts was the high standard achieved in every branch of Festival work. Peter Ebert, whom my brother had met during his visits to Glyndebourne Opera, was our producer during our second year, and for many years after. I don't believe we have ever bettered him. He was a kind person who appreciated that our chorus – all locals – would be a bit nervous; in fact, two of our girls, daunted by the prospect of facing a stranger with such a reputation, asked me to tell him that they would prefer to be in the back row or behind the biggest rock on the stage. I wasn't very hopeful of being able to engineer that, being over-awed myself, but during a break in Peter's first production rehearsal I noticed the same two girls in animated conversation with him. He was a wonderful producer, and one for whom we would all have stood on our heads if asked. Indeed, one year when another producer fell ill and my brother had asked Peter if he could help in

Left: *Anthony Besch is one of the most distinguished post-war producers, starting his career under Carl Ebert at Glyndebourne. He first came to Wexford to produce the 1955 operas (*Manon Lescaut *and* Der Wildschütz*) and returned for four further seasons –* Mireille *(1961),* Otello *(1967),* La Rondine *(1971) and* Oberon *(1972).*

Centre: *An early portrait of the popular Genoese tenor Ugo Benelli, whose Wexford appearances range from the 1965 production of Mozart's* La Finta Giardiniera *to a series of memorable celebrity recitals in the 1980s.*

Myer Fredman conducted the 1966 production of Auber's Fra Diavolo *and returned to Wexford for* Luisa Miller *(1969) and* La Rondine *(1971).*

the emergency, he agreed, but because his time was restricted he hoped that we could work late a few nights. The response was unanimous: if it meant staying up all night we would be available!

L'Elisir d'Amore was our first Italian opera, and to help with the language we had Father Enda, OFM, who gave up his free time to try and make us sound mellifluous in the Italian style. This he did for the years he was in Wexford, and when we wandered into German, French or other foreign opera, there was always some expert to help us with our language difficulties.

Standards in other ways were high too. Regulations had

to be followed, not only by the local singers but by professional chorus members who were employed during later years. For instance, a lady hired in Glyndebourne to sing a specific line in the chorus announced she had already sung a different line in another production and was sticking to it. My brother then presented the spokesperson for the visiting chorus group with the ultimatum: 'Either Miss ___ learns the line she was told to by the next rehearsal or she can collect her return boat-ticket for the following night at the office.' She learned the line and was no further trouble.

Down the years we have had many wonderful workers attached to the Festival. Most were locals of course, and many of them voluntary! The late Eugene McCarthy gave us the use of rooms in his hotel, where he and his wife Maureen and his secretary Doreen, boosted by some of us, would work at the bookings until late at night. Dr Des Ffrench, with the help of Dr Jim Liddy, took responsibility for recitals, choral performances and the wonderful opera and ballet films which were a feature of the early years. Des was instrumental in giving us the chance to host the great Hallé Orchestra under its conductor Sir John Barbirolli, and one of the early performances of the St James's Gate Choir under the late Victor Leeson. Séamus O'Dwyer, a great anchor man and a dedicated opera follower, was ever ready to lend a hand backstage or front of house when necessary, as were so many others.

Our first connection with Italy and Italians was through Nicola Monti and Elvira Ramelli. Christiano Dallamangas was Greek, so Italian for him was a stage language, and he had no English. One of my local colleagues was able to tell me that Dallamangas had two children who lived with his wife in Greece, and he was hoping that they would not take to the stage; I asked how he had come upon such information, given that Dallamangas had no English and my friend had no Greek and just enough knowledge of Italian to learn his words. My friend thought for a moment and said, 'I think it was by signs'.

Nicola Monti was a great favourite in Wexford, although despite his many visits he did not learn a word of English, and he didn't need it. At a time when you could become an Associate Member of the Opera for a few shillings, with the right to attend rehearsals, a friend of mine listened to Monti sing 'Una Furtiva Lagrima', and said: 'When he sings like that, wouldn't you give him sixpence and boil milk for him.'

We have had some marvellous designers, particularly Joseph Carl in the early days, and Reggie Woolley, whose quality in perspective made the stage grow under his brush. During the production of *Lucrezia Borgia* (1966) in which there was no ladies' chorus, I coaxed my way into the lighting box, then situated at the back of the Circle. From there the set looked like a long hall of at least fifty yards. Woolley had also designed and painted an equally impressive set for *La Gioconda* (1963), which did have a ladies' chorus, and even on the stage we were impressed with the staircases and buildings he had conjured up.

In those early days we had to face many a jibe about our Theatre Royal. It had been in poor condition for years, as it was seldom used. Baritone Paola Pedani had great fun on discovering that when he poked his fingers through the so-called 'wall' of a downstairs dressingroom, he could amuse himself by looking through while waiting to go on stage. The 'wall' was canvas covered by a light, crumbling plaster. However, our greatest worry was the year the great John Pritchard was due as our conductor. He was director of the Liverpool Philharmonic Orchestra that had played for us in 1961, when the Radio Éireann Symphony wasn't free to attend Wexford. We waited with bated breath for the great man's comments about the theatre. Although it had undergone some reconstruction the previous year (mainly the addition of dressing rooms), we knew it was well below the standards of any theatres he or his orchestra had visited. I watched him at our first rehearsal dusting the ledge where he sat in beautiful pale grey slacks, and waited for the worst. Would he go back on the next boat? Our friend Séamus O'Dwyer, who had been appointed to bring this great man back to the hotel after the rehearsal, knew we'd be waiting for news, and he returned to assure us that the only thing Pritchard talked of was the excellent work by an amateur chorus. We were very relieved!

I think it was that same year that my forethought paid dividends. In any production there may be many cuts — short sections taken out of the scores by arrangement with conductor and producer — but that year there was a doubt about one whole chorus. I thought it was safer to learn the piece, but I wasn't popular, as this meant staying on a few minutes later than the full rehearsal, it being a 'ladies only' chorus. At the first production rehearsal our stage director announced that this chorus was now reinstated.

When he asked how many chorus members had rehearsed it, only the local girls could give a show of hands, and they were sufficient in number for that scene. My reputation was saved.

The bass Franco Ventriglia and baritone Lino Puglisi were a wonderful duo who actually met at the Festival. I believe their most famous performance was a duet in *I Puritani* (1962). It received a greater encore each night than any performance I can recall. That year we were also fortunate to have Mirelli Freni play a dramatic role which she had been hoping to do for a long time. She was subsequently called upon by opera buffs from all over the world to do this type of performance.

1965 was an extraordinary year. We had three operas – *La Traviata* (Verdi) produced by Peter Ebert, *Don Quichotte* (Massenet) produced by Carl Ebert, Peter's father, and *La Finta Giardiniera* (Mozart) also produced by Peter Ebert, with costumes and settings designed by Judith Ebert, Peter's daughter. Three generations of the one famous family working together in Wexford! Peter had been with us a couple of times during the summer, checking the length of the Mozart opera. As it was to be an afternoon performance, some cuts were necessary, though this was difficult in the absence of a chorus. Peter decided to tighten up a lot of the recitative content, and he asked me to ensure that the musical element was smoothly rejoined. I'm pleased to say that there were no signs of breaks or joints when the performance got going, and I'm sure the conductor and orchestra never realised that a mere chorus member 'let loose' on a Mozart score had made the changes.

A very special performance by a producer who actually took part in the production itself brings me to another highlight. Sesto Bruscantini came to Wexford in 1977 with an excellent reputation for acting and producing. In his first opera here, which was one of a Triple Bill of Comedies, he took the part of 'Il Maestro di Cappello' (Cimarosa). This was the most brilliant performance of mime I have ever seen – one man alone on the stage with a few props, no speech, no singing, only his expressive face and quirky movement against a musical background. I discovered a few years later that he was to produce *Un Giorno di Regio* (Verdi) with the visiting chorus only, so I asked our artistic director of that time, Adrian Slack, if I might also take part in it. Because I had retired from business and was living on my own I could have as much time for the extra rehearsals as the professionals. He very kindly let me take part. This was another bonus that resulted from 'being on hand'.

I've mentioned only a handful of the real friends of the Festival in Wexford, and their marvellous help and support. There were also the backstage workers, scenery painters, tea-makers, programme sellers, ushers and box office personnel, and of course Miss Mai McElroy who worked with Reggie Woolley on design. Naturally my first love is with my stage colleagues, the chorus members whom I was privileged to join; and even after the most recent audition, last year, I was still passed as 'of acceptable standard' thanks to our present artistic director. In addition to all this, a new generation of young singers are now my very kind and helpful companions – it's not everyone would put up with a chorus member who is older than her own parents! Children of some of our first chorus members are now taking part in performances. Many of our visiting artists have early connections with the Festival; quite a few have studied under Laura Sarti, for many years an excellent member of the visiting artists. A recent principal studied under the famous Bruscantini, and another, a soprano, not alone studied under our dear Marlyn Cotlow of *La Sonnambula*, but is also her daughter-in-law. These connections show that the Wexford Festival Opera is still a thriving institution. There are many more people I should no doubt have mentioned, but all I can say is – how lucky I was to be born in Wexford and how privileged to take part in such a venture.

L'Elisir d'Amore

'Gramophone Musicians'

by Norris Davidson

Having joined Radio Éireann in the 1940s, Norris Davidson *was assigned the task of introducing the first Festival production to wireless listeners in 1951. Since then he has beguiled his audiences with the wit and erudition of his commentaries every season. He continues to write and direct memorable television documentaries on subjects ranging from the painter Derek Hill, a long-standing Festival Council member, to the legends surrounding the seals which bask around the Wexford coast.*

Having achieved such success in the 1952 production of L'Elisir d'Amore, *Cristiano Dallamangas and Nicola Monti are seen 'preparing' for the 1953 presentation of Donizetti's other great comedy* Don Pasquale.

A stalwart of early Festivals was Bryan Balkwill who conducted the 1953 opera Don Pasquale *and returned for the 1954, 1955, 1956, 1957, 1958 and 1961 — nine operas in all.*

The Festival is almost unthinkable without Ballinrobe-born Courtney Kenny who has served on the music staff for many years as well as presenting his own inimitable late-night shows and accompanying countless recitals and concerts.

Elaine Padmore, who became the Festival's fifth artistic director in 1982.

The first word I ever read about the proposed Festival in Wexford was typed on a memo that was hand-delivered to my room in Radio Éireann, forerunner to the present Radio Telefís Éireann and then located at the top of the GPO, Dublin. I read that the Festival would include an Irish production of the opera *The Rose of Castile*, to be produced in the autumn by one of the Radio Éireann Players, John Stephenson, in conjunction with the Radio Éireann Light Orchestra conducted by Dermot O'Hara. I read on. I was to make a radio documentary about the opera and all the activity that surrounded it. It was the desire of Dr Tom Walsh that the opera should be presented in the manner of the *commedia dell'arte* . To have converted the rather stodgy *Rose* into such a soufflé would have been beyond any operatic producer of the day, and it certainly was beyond John Stephenson, who was no musician. Dr Walsh ground out the words 'If John Stephenson's going to produce it he'll produce it in the manner of the comedy dell' John Stephenson'. In the end it was produced by the amiable and experienced Harry Powell-Lloyd, who also produced the following year's *L'Elisir d'Amore*.

The fact that Radio Éireann choose an actor and stage-producer for this opera shows that they really regarded the Wexford effort as a sort of amateur *Rose,* to be associated with *Marie* rather than the pure Castilian variety, deserving of benevolent support rather than professional attention. However, Dr Tom's insistence on the appointment of Powell-Lloyd over and above the Dublin choice was a definite mark of progress in his operatic apprenticeship.

As none of my letters was ever answered, I went to Wexford to see Dr Walsh. There was a steeliness about him in those days, especially noticeable around the mouth and eyes, and although he must have had many doubts and fears, he was a man who showed nothing but faith and determination that the opera would succeed. Even during the very first production, he was thinking ahead to the next opera but one (*Don Pasquale*, though he didn't name it then); he led by his fearless conviction that opera *was* going to follow opera. He was also a man who could delegate, as one of the anecdotes passed round at his funeral shows. It concerned a director of the chorus who complained to him about some of its members. Walsh's reply was immediate: 'I know, why do you think I put you in charge?'

I never wrote to him again, as one was expected to answer one's own questions, although I did have some letters from him: invitations, Christmas cards and thank you notes...things like that. He was always a very pleasant host, especially renowned for his famous Sunday morning sessions during the season. But the general operatic plan was always there, and I know that he resented having to depend on Radio Éireann for the music, as he would not have complete command of it. He once told me crossly that he was thinking of getting the Boyd-Neel orchestra in, and in the end he did engage part of an English orchestra. However, its members seemed mainly to regard the visit as a holiday in jolly old Éire, and enjoyed it in such a fashion that sometimes orchestra, singers and conductor all abandoned posts and went their own jolly old ways.

During the first two to three years, artists sometimes sang after the performance in local bars, enjoying themselves and delighting the customers. Tom Walsh stopped all that. He felt that it wasn't suitable opera season behaviour, that somehow it cheapened the festival season, and in spite of the fact that this annoyed some people, he was probably right. This same determination made him disregard proposals to revive 'prime old favourites' to follow *The Rose of Castile*, and pursue instead the current Wexford policy of presenting unusual works that are not commonly heard.

The Rose of Castile was revived again in 1991 for a spring weekend, but it somehow lacked the atmosphere of the first Festival production. The town was no longer cautious and suspicious, there was little curiosity and the lane leading up to the theatre was no longer lined with people standing at their doors applauding the long dresses and display. Television and a general familiarity have erased the novelty of the early days. Things have simply changed. In 1951 the auditorium was different, and the backstage area had something medieval about it — something that suggested a morality play put on in the open air of an inn yard. There were creaking wooden stairs that led to a gallery and a few hutches grandiosely described as 'dressing rooms'. The cold was truly medieval, a special cold that had been retained from Wexford's early history and was now being re-distributed. For the first few years some of the artists, like Mirella Freni, even dressed in their hotel rooms and cabbed to the theatre. A far cry from the Theatre Royal of today.

But there are other differences too. Then, a line drawn from horn to horn of the Circle would have coincided more or less with the front of the orchestral space; I say 'space' because there was no real pit. The black and gold proscenium of today was the back of the stage, and that was the back of the building. If you stepped out of what is a box today, you would be walking past the ancient dimmer-board (that has its own history) and onto the stage. The front of the stage was a wooden wall with a door that was used by the band. Behind the wall and in the neighbourhood of some coke was a trestle-table that held the recording equipment operated by Aidan Folan, in short earshot of the music and the feet and voices overhead.

Some years later we moved to a cold, high and dangerous roof-top area, once a film projection-room, which gave a view of the stage so postage-stamp small that it seemed altogether unconnected with the sounds the microphones brought up out of it. After several years perched there we moved to a room about a third of the way up the Circle but outside the auditorium and looking into it. We were assured that this grim cavern would be done up — maybe even the cold walls of bare stone would be plastered. One does not have a Proustian wish for cork lining, but just for a simple transformation — to make it suitable for something like, say, the broadcasting of opera. Pray for us!

The Wexford theatre is a pin-drop theatre; a whisper can be heard at the back of the Circle, something that many singers do not take in until after a few performances. This quality gives the voice back to an artist in a very encouraging way, but it caused great problems at the first Wexford operas. It was not that the orchestra could not play quietly, but that its conductor would not allow it to, and Dermot O'Hara was as enthusiastic a pioneer as any in those days. He insisted that if the orchestra were quieter its sound would not expand and develop, that regardless of the acoustic compass of the theatre, the orchestra's sound must be allowed to mature. Develop and mature it did — at the smallest indication of an *f* the band was so driven that the bare walls slammed it from side to side.

Those who heard the revival (I was brought up to 'hear' an opera, rather than 'see' it) of *The Rose of Castile* will remember the travesty role of a girl called Carmen. The laughs at the end of her arietta were underlined so strongly on Dermot O'Hara's instruction, that the theatre seemed to rock. On being asked to play more quietly, to give the girl an opportunity of being heard, he pleaded development of the musical sound. He had no idea of what the echo was doing to it, and Dr Walsh himself intervened. The conductor afterwards mentioned 'gramophone musicians', preceded by an adjective that, as he used it, defied analysis. In the end there was a compromise that was rather in Dermot's favour.

Opera productions have their troubles but in Wexford they do not last; Dr Walsh continued to let Dermot O'Hara rehearse soloists at his piano and in his house. He probably did not hear the comment 'gramophone musicians', and even if he did hear it, he would not have allowed mere words to interfere with the presentation of music.

Improvisation wasn't often the name of the game in those days, but on one occasion a piano I found in the theatre (not Dr Walsh's) was going to have to be adapted to provide a harpsichord *continuo* for *Don Pasquale* by having drawing pins pushed into its hammers. Even though the piano may have had nothing to do with Radio Éireann, I protested that, as every child knows, pushing down the sustaining pedal and then sliding lavatory paper between hammers and strings, certainly changes the tone of the instrument into something rich and strange. I don't know what happened in the end but that was the only time I found anything being cobbled together for the occasion; somehow whatever we needed always turned up.

In forty years I never heard anyone despair about the Wexford opera's future, though coming out from more than forty performances I have heard people wondering how it could continue and expressing their gratitude that they had heard some of the operas before the house darkened. But I never noticed the organisers feeling that the end was nigh. Naturally there has been nervousness because opera is a business that never pays, but difficulties are always overcome with a steely determination not found anywhere other than this bottom right-hand corner of Ireland.

Reminiscences

by Nicky Cleary

A long-serving member of the voluntary backstage crew,
Nicky Cleary *is today regarded as the key person in ensuring that each production appears on the tiny stage on time and just as the designer envisaged it. As the Festival stage director he has to cope with the Theatre Royal's limited facilities and small storage area, and does so with a remarkable calm and practical skill, season after season.*

The distinguished cast of the 1958 production of Donizetti's Anna Bolena *included Marina Cucchio (Anna), Plinio Clabassi (Henry VIII) and Fiorenza Cossotto (Jane Seymour).*

Dr Tom Walsh often told of how the idea of running an opera festival in Wexford occurred to him while he was in a bookshop. It could be said that the idea of becoming involved backstage with the same Festival occurred to me also in a shop – a record shop. A friend and I had begun collecting records and we went every Saturday to the same little shop in the Selskar area of the town to buy or order those precious opera records. At the shop we invariably met people who were very much involved in the opera Festival. Among them was Seamus O'Dwyer, one of the co-founders with Dr Walsh, and until his untimely death, Dr Tom's right-hand man. We often bumped into Dessie McDonald, then stage manager. It was Dessie who suggested to us that

we should come to work backstage in the theatre. The idea appealed to both of us and we became involved. My friend left after a year or two but I am still there and, like Edith Piaf, have no regrets.

Working backstage was both exciting and satisfying. What an opportunity it presented to a young fellow interested in opera, living in a small town in Ireland, to be able to hear and watch at close quarters world famous artists in rehearsal and performance! It could only have happened in Wexford and because of one man – Dr Tom Walsh. Year after year Dr Tom, or as he was known to his stage crew 'Il Dottore', brought wonderful voices to Wexford. I still recall the opening passage in a review of one of the Festivals in *Opera*, which posed the question,

'Why is it that Wexford hears them first, Glyndebourne hears them second and then Covent Garden?' Monti, Calabrese, Freni, Cossotto, Adani, Tadeo, Trama, Fissore, Nordin, Pedani, Nicolov…the list goes on and on. Indeed, Wexford can still beat them to it: Sergei Leiferkus, Ljubomir Videnov, Alessandra Marc, Carla Lavani, Raul Giminez, to mention just a few.

It is strange that the incidents which remain most vividly in one's memory are those from earlier Festivals: how Monti used to wait inside the stage door after each performance for the car to take him back to his hotel, his mouth and the lower part of his face wrapped in a large white towel; how Professor Carl Ebert, producer of *Don Quichotte*, would always stoop down and touch the wood of the stage immediately on entering the theatre every night: his son Peter told us that he did that in every opera house he worked in around the world.

One remembers the very moving death scene in *Don Quichotte*, with Miroslav Cangalovic in the title role and Ladko Korosec as Sancho. During every performance two members of the National Ballet could be seen sitting on the floor in the wings, their chins on their knees and tears streaming down their faces as they watched the scene and listened to Massenet's glorious music, gloriously sung and gloriously played. Then there was the great Marko Rothmüller in *Manon Lescaut*, standing centre stage just behind the curtain during the lovely intermezzo before Act III, conducting the music as though he was the conductor, having first turned to the chorus with a finger to his lips, saying: 'Quiet please, there is music'. Franco Calabrese, the bass with the voice like 'pure velvet', in *La Sonnambula* would be waiting in the wings to make the Sign of the Cross with his left hand. During the 1963 revival of *Don Pasquale*, which was not considered to be an outstanding success, I remember waiting in the wings during every rehearsal and performance to hear Alfonz Bartha's beautiful singing of 'Sogno soave'. In more recent times who can forget Sergei Leiferkus singing the 'Ballad of the Sage Book' in the 1984 *Le Jongleur de Notre Dame*?

Such are some of the memories and some of the bonuses of working backstage at the Wexford Festival Opera.

Opposite: *A remarkable group of young singers was assembled for the 1957 Donizetti opera* La Figlia del Reggimento, *including Gwyn Griffiths, Patricia Kern, Graziella Sciutti, Mario Spina and Geraint Evans.*

Above: *Miroslav Cangalovic made a great impression on the 1965 presentation of Massenet's* Don Quichotte.

The Theatre Royal, Wexford

A chronicle rather than a history
by Barbara Wallace and Seán O'Laoire

Barbara Wallace *was elected chairman of Wexford Festival Opera Council in 1986. She has been a voluntary worker and Council member since 1967.* **Seán O'Laoire,** *partner in Murray O'Laoire Associates, was consulting architect with Albert Lennon for the 1987 theatre extension. The firm is the recipient of a number of national awards and won the Europa Nostre Award for the rehabilitation of Lord Limerick's house in Limerick.*

Wexford Theatre Royal was built in 1830 in High Street by William Taylor and opened for the first time to the public in 1832.

An earlier theatre in Church Lane is said to have 'failed to flourish', and there is no evidence to support local folklore concerning an even earlier theatre in the Cornmarket. It is thought that musical and dramatic performances given in the Assembly Rooms — now the Wexford Arts Centre — may well be the basis of this belief.

The Theatre Royal was built before such luxuries as coal gas, and was lighted by candles and oil. There is no record as to how the house was heated but the local paper in 1886 'complained in public of its bitter, biting and insufferable draughts'.

In his article on provincial theatres in Ireland, Christopher Fitz-Simon says that the Theatre Royal in Wexford is the nearest we have to the traditional 18th-century arrangement of deep forestage and proscenium door. He points out that this in reality is the result of the 1961 restoration work which makes it appear that the building is older than is actually the case.

There are unconfirmed reports that the theatre seated 700 when it was built. If this were true, it would have been quite large by the standards of that time. London's Drury Lane Theatre, before its rebuilding in 1775, seated 750 people.

Because few towns in Ireland had regular theatre, patrons came to Wexford from a wide radius and travelled by the old style stagecoaches.

It was not unusual for music lovers to attend the theatre six nights a week when the Walsham Grand Opera Season was running in Wexford. Many talented companies, with principals from Covent Garden, His Majesty's, and Drury Lane Theatre, London, played regular seasons. The people of the town were reputed to be keenly appreciative of fine music and critical in their judgements regarding it.

From the early 1900s, Wexford's Amateur Light Opera Society performed annually at the Theatre Royal, as they do today.

Lord Longford, Hilton Edwards, Micheál MacLiammóir and Anew McMaster were amongst the many who played at the Wexford Theatre Royal regularly. McMaster in particular was a staunch admirer of the building and loved the Wexford audiences.

A letterhead of the theatre at that period tells us that it was on 'Direct line of tour and within easy distance of Dublin, Waterford, Cork and Limerick, with bi-weekly sailings to Liverpool — weekly to Bristol — twice daily to Fishguard, from Wexford Quays'.

The proprietor and manager at that time was Edward P Ronan. His daughter, Ellen Ronan Goodall (Barbara Wallace's mother) was the last private owner of the theatre. It was sold by her in 1942 to a consortium of Wexford businessmen for use as a cinema.

Two family documents are to be seen in the Ronan Room off the upper balcony: one is a contract signed by Hilaire Belloc, lecturer, author and Parliamentarian, to give a lecture in Wexford's Theatre Royal on 1 November 1910, for the sum of 10 guineas. The other document is a claim for seating and scenery damaged by fire in 1926, where one can read that tip-up seats were to be replaced at 12/6 each. These seats are still in use today. It is interesting to note that at that time there were 40 seats in boxes in the theatre.

The 1942 renovations

In 1942 the Theatre Royal was completely remodelled as

a cinema, but the name was retained, as was the stage, so that professional and amateur groups could still perform. The chief structural alteration was the removal of the upper circle and the installation of the steeply raked balcony which has now been extended.

In the souvenir programme for the reopening that year, we are told with pride that 'The old Boxes and Gallery have been swept away and in their stead is the new Balcony with tier on tier of dark crimson seats from each one of which is a perfect view of stage and screen. Carpeted oak stairways lead to these seats. The fine acoustics of the old building have now been exploited to the full by the installation of the world-famous Western Electric Mirrophonic Sound. Patrons may confidently expect one hundred percent perfection of sound'. Christopher Fitz-Simon describes the modernisation in a slightly different way (see page 51).

The modern theatre

Having acquired the theatre in the 1950s, the Festival Council gradually cleaned and repaired the building. In 1961, with help from the Calouste Gulbenkian Foundation and the Irish Tourist Board, the backstage area was enlarged and the proscenium arch rebuilt to a classical design by D O'Neill Flanagan. A small adjoining house in High Street was bought in 1973 for offices, wardrobe and storage. Further building took place in 1979 when extra dressing rooms, showers and lighting equipment were added under the guiding hand of Albert Lennon.

We can see then that the auditorium, which has housed the Festival since the 1950s, has a chequered past. How then does one approach the design of yet another significant modification? It would not be an overstatement, or an insult, to observe that the Theatre Royal lacks many of the archetypal features of the 'Opera House' — tiered balconies, boxes and efflorescent baroque plasterwork. What it lacks in architectural pedigree is compensated by eclectic and intimate charm.

Integrity of style was not always of primary concern to opera house architects. Indeed the eccentric Victorian Frank Matcham — possibly the most prolific theatre and opera house designer in architectural history — would often place a fantastic Hinduesque elephant head, cheek (or trunk) by jowl with a cherub, an achantus leaf and a bastard Corinthian capital, with little scruple! His work for the Grand Opera House, Belfast, is a fine example of his riotous imagination.

Old Wexford hands will appreciate the factors that have determined the form of this latest change in the form of the building. The house is land locked and incapable of expansion in any direction except skywards — hence the dramatic cantilever structure housing the upper seating levels of the extended circle. This expansion provides for the bulk of the additional seats, the balance being provided by colonising the space previously occupied by the 'kink' on the rear right of the stalls.

The most radical change however in the form of the house is undoubtedly in the ceiling. The addition of 100-odd souls and the increased area required to house them was found to upset the volumetric and spatial equation that would have ensured the maintenance of the acoustic performance of the building. Additional volume to offset increased absorption, in a form that would ensure proper reflection and diffusion of sound, was required.

The roof space, for long the happy home of generations of pigeons, was invaded to reveal magnificent king post trusses. The germ of a design resolution was at hand. The A-roof profile which now envelopes the house is close to being an ideal acoustic ceiling form. The coffered fibrous plaster mouldings which are planted on the ceiling between trusses assist in the diffusion of sound. The new roof form can be seen as an acoustic expedient. It is much more than that. It reveals history and structural essence, connecting and binding all the changes that have shaped the Theatre Royal since its foundation.

The detailing of the space, the painting and colour of walls, the gilding of the truss champhers, grew out of the resolution of design problems. In doing so they recognise the eclectic grammar of the embellishment of the space from previous generations: O'Neill-Flanagan's Neo-classical Proscenium frame, the (still vacant) statuary plinths, the vestigial 'box' mouldings and the curved plaster uplighter boxes, the lighting cupola, the brass rails, are designed in the same spirit and maintain a dialogue with the past.

This was the design intent: to blend the familiar with the new and the revealed essence of the theatre roof structure. The new product may still defy stylistic classification. This is not said apologetically. Opera-going has its rituals and the auditorium must provide the *mise-en-scène*. Frank Matcham knew this as did his antecedents. In lighter moments during the design process it was postulated that we may have contrived a new style – 'peasant baroque'.

Stylish pedigree must then be seen in the perspective of the history of the theatre and in relation to the constraints that governed these latest changes. Wexford's unique standing as an international venue for opera is testimony to a range of qualities: the intimacy and charm of the venue, the quality of the product, and the setting – Wexford and her people, which combine to provide the ingredients of memory. The new extension and modifications it is to be hoped will contribute to the perpetuation of the success of the Festival and in doing so welcome many new friends. In conclusion and in celebration of this phase of the theatre's history we can truly rejoice and sing: 'let the rafters ring'.

Dr Patrick Hillery, President of Ireland (1976-1990), discussing the operas with Festival chairman Seán Scallan (1971-1976).

Scenes that are brightest: Provincial theatres in Ireland

by Christoper Fitz-Simon

Christopher Fitz-Simon *first visited Wexford during the fourth Festival when he was producer and member of the cast of a Dublin University Players' midnight revue. He moved into the world of theatre and television directing, and for a time was a member of the Wexford Festival Council and the Repertoire Committee. He is author of several books on the arts in Ireland, and has updated his article, which originally appeared in the 1977 programme.*

The first public theatre in Ireland was situated in Werburgh Street, Dublin. Theatrical performances had taken place elsewhere, but this was the first recognisable theatre building; it was opened in 1637, with John Ogilby as Master of the Revels. Another, subsequently more celebrated, was erected in Smock Alley a few hundred yards away, in 1662. Cork's first theatre was opened in 1736, and Belfast's in 1793. The latter stood at the corner of Arthur Street and Castle Lane — many Belfast people will remember the Royal Cinema on that site, a direct descendant of the first theatre, and only demolished a few years ago.

Theatres opened and closed with astonishing rapidity in all three cities. Dublin at least enjoyed a reasonable continuity of performance from the early 18th century, and Ireland in general became a theatrical training-ground, particularly for authors, whose works have adorned the English-speaking theatre from Farquhar to Beckett. It is not the purpose of this paper to dwell on the personalities, or their activities, but rather on the theatre buildings of the smaller cities. A considerable amount of activity existed in the 'provinces', although the scene was a far cry from the glitter of what we are wont to imagine prevailed 200 years ago; and the theatres of Dublin were hardly less ramshackle and unhygienic than those of the county towns.

Architectural developments in theatre building

The nearest we have in Ireland to the traditional 18th-century arrangement of deep forestage and proscenium-door is in Wexford — though in fact this is the result of the 1961 restoration which visually credits the Theatre Royal as being much older than is actually the case. The early theatres were quite small: even London's famous Theatre Royal in Drury Lane would only have seated 750 persons to modern standards of comfort prior to the rebuilding by Adam in 1775 — of course several hundred more were probably crammed in on the benches. The usual shape was a semi-circle with boxes extending over the forestage *(pro-scenium)*. Behind this was the proscenium-arch and curtain dividing the public part of the house from the stage *(scenium)*. Proscenium-doors on either side of the stage (Wexford has only one) enabled the actors to make entrances in front of the curtain or drop-scene.

The 18th-century performer had the advantage of experiencing the audience at very close quarters; a naturalistic type of acting had therefore evolved, and David Garrick was its chief exponent. Soon after Garrick's death in 1779 new building techniques enabled theatres to be greatly expanded — roof-spans were widened, fly-towers raised; stages were made deeper, the forestage disappeared, and the larger orchestra-pit created a division between actor and audience.

As the 19th century progressed, the architect and engineer exercised undue influence, and dramatist and performer were forced into attempting to achieve their effects with bolder strokes, so to speak; subtlety was gone for a burthen, and spectacle (including opera) came into its own. Until the close of the 19th century when, as a result of the fresh breezes from Norway, smaller theatres more suitable for drama were again constructed, dramatic writing, and probably acting, reached its lowest ebb. (In Dublin, intimacy was reintroduced by the Irish Literary Theatre and other groups in the nineties, culminating in the opening of the Abbey Theatre in 1903).

Because of small populations, and a persisting absence of finance, Ireland's provincial 18th-century theatres remained small in spite of the trends abroad, serving the needs of music-hall variety, operetta, burlesque and entertainments composed of jugglers, hypnotists and sword-swallowers, as much as of companies engaged in purveying grand opera, drama, or diversions of a classier kind.

The visits of the Smock Alley Players to Newry became so popular that a permanent theatre was built there in 1769. Limerick's first theatre was erected by Tottenham Heaphy in 1770. In 1773 a theatre was opened in Drogheda and in 1774 in Derry. There are references to a theatre existing in Galway in 1783, but the site is not known. Even much smaller towns, like Ballinasloe and Tralee, possessed purpose-built theatres by the mid-19th century. It must be assumed that these were extremely modest in scale and in style.

The Kilkenny Theatre

In 1802 Richard Power of Kilfane founded the Kilkenny Theatre. His company, an amateur one of what must have been considerable talent and perseverance, gave a season every year until 1819. The plays were most imaginatively chosen and were probably unusually well set and dressed due to the social standing of the participants. In 1808 the Kilkenny artist John Comerford, who was to become an important portrait painter, published a portfolio of likenesses of the players, many of whom were members of the Power family. The Theatre was situated on the Parade opposite the Castle gardens. This site has often been confused with that of a later Kilkenny Theatre, one of the many examples of the munificence of the widow of the fourth Lord Desart, in Patrick Street (again, not to be confused with the Desart Hall). Lady Desart bestowed a building but not a management, and the theatre never really flourished. Throughout the 1930s and '40s sporadic visits by professional companies interspersed the annual production of the Ossory Players and an ever-engulfing programme of far from high-class cinema. Kilkenny was not regarded as a 'good date' by the touring companies. When the theatre came on the market recently there was not sufficient local endeavour to save it, and the city lost an undistinguished though serviceable house exactly at the time when national opera, ballet, and drama companies started a new era in touring in the present decade. The

auditorium still exists, so there is still a possibility of salvation.

The Theatre Royal, Waterford

The only truly traditional theatres which remain in operation outside Dublin are those of Waterford and Wexford. The Theatre Royal, Waterford, is much the more interesting architecturally. There was a theatre in Bedford Street which opened in 1788, but as the new City Hall of the same date contained Assembly Rooms in which all kinds of delightful entertainments took place, it probably died from superior competition. The architect of the City Hall, John Roberts, may be described as the most gifted local architect of the century – 'local' in the sense that as far as is known he never worked outside his native city, to which he also gave two handsome cathedrals and the superb Chamber of Commerce. Roberts' Assembly Rooms were altered and renamed 'Theatre Royal' in 1876. There is a story to the effect that the model was the Gaiety in Dublin, and though it is possible that the same architect was employed, the two theatres could hardly be more different. The Theatre Royal is basically 18th-century both in plan and section; the Gaiety's low-slung dress circle, unaligned with the upper gallery, and its heavy Victorian decoration, contrasts (unfavourably, I think) with the sedate symmetry of Waterford.

The Theatre Royal, Waterford, was visited by many distinguished companies, a preponderance of them bearing the impressive billing *Cross-Channel*. By an unfortunate decision of the Corporation the house was later leased to a cinema management, and though stage productions continued, as in Kilkenny, the auditorium was allowed to deteriorate to a condition where the local appellation 'flea-pit' was perfectly well deserved. The Corporation, to its eternal shame, would have converted the theatre into offices, were it not that certain citizens raised funds from industry, the Irish Tourist Board, and private persons, towards its reinstatement. The remainder of Roberts' City Hall now requires the same sympathetic renovatory attention.

The Theatre Royal, Wexford

The Theatre Royal, Wexford, was opened in 1830 by Mr William Taylor, an earlier theatre having failed to flourish in Church Lane. Dr T J Walsh has written that there is no evidence to support a local tradition concerning an even earlier one in the Cornmarket. It is quite probable, however, that some sort of musical or dramatic performances were given in the old (1775) Assembly Rooms, now the Wexford Arts Centre, in the Cornmarket – and this may have caused confusion in the public memory. Traditions of this kind die hard, and there is another to the effect that a theatre stood in the vicinity of Spawell Road, but maps do not seem to corroborate.

In 1832 a Wexford artist, John Wills, painted a drop-scene depicting the River Slaney at Ferrycarrig. This was evidently the theatre's main adornment; it was repainted many times and is still remembered by a few erstwhile patrons. Various companies played here, though no great celebrities: Wexford was, it seems, a 'second run' house on the touring circuit, until Anew McMaster founded his Shakespeare Company in the 1920s. McMaster came regularly to Wexford for the next quarter-century; he was a staunch admirer of the building and of the audiences. The Wexford Amateur Operatic Society – ancestor of the excellent Light Opera Society – performed here regularly from the early 1900s. 'Living Pictures' were exhibited in the 1920s; and gradually the cinema took over, as happened everywhere else.

The Theatre Royal was completely remodelled as a cinema in 1942, but the name was retained, as was the stage, so that professional and amateur groups could perform from time to time. Wexford has always maintained a number of amateur drama, operatic, and choral groups, and in this way the movies never destroyed the continuity of live theatre. The chief structural alteration was the removal of the upper circle and the installation of the steeply-raked balcony which we know today. On entering the auditorium the habitué would have been most forcibly struck by the absence of the Ferrycarrig scene and the replacement of the old proscenium arch by a cardboardy structure partly inspired by the dying embers of *art-deco* (which seems to have reached Wexford rather later than elsewhere) and partly by that Moorish style favoured by the architects of Alhambras and Granadas from Tuam to Tooting. This remarkable scheme was continued in stipple throughout the foyer, where the bemused patron might pause to observe some curved steps in slime-green terrazo.

It was not unnatural that when the first Wexford Festival opera was presented in 1951 the decorations, *démodé* even when executed, seemed utterly inappropriate – the more so, as the plaster and paint had not been well maintained. For the first Festival, a Mrs O'Connor manufactured several thousand chrysanthemums from paper, in order to conceal the worst cracks.

Having taken over the management of the theatre in 1951, the Festival Council gradually cleaned and repaired the building with what I can only describe as loving care. In 1961, with help from the Calouste Gulbenkian Foundation and the Irish Tourist Board, the backstage area was enlarged and the proscenium arch rebuilt to a classical design by D O'Neill Flanagan which caused much controversy, many people feeling that this was just as much a fake as the Mauresque excesses of the 1940s; but to me it seems to be totally in the right spirit, considering the period of the original shell of the house, and the proportions of stage and auditorium. Later, four small adjoining houses in High Street were acquired, for administration, wardrobe and workrooms of various kinds. The further enlargement of the theatre in 1988, by Seán O'Laoire for Albert Lennon, also seems to me to be entirely appropriate; the extended balcony, with its exposed and painted beams, provides a stunning panorama of the orchestra and proscenium, and a sense of visual excitement before the curtain even begins to rise on the operatic scene. The north-facing façades of the houses have been left as they were, preserving the domestic harmony of this most charming street.

Johnstown Castle is a favourite place to visit during the Festival as it is situated a few miles from the town.

Wexford and Loch Garman

by Nicholas Furlong

No one could have taken on the mantle of the late George Haddon better than Nicholas Furlong *who organises the historical and archaeological tours of the town and county each year. These tours are a highlight of the Wexford Festival for many visitors and have been copied by other festivals in recent times.*

'The saga of Wexford begins far back in the mists of prehistory'.

That profound verdict by Hadden defies contradiction. The dilemma which Wexford presents to those who would explain it was once made evident by the founder of the Old Wexford Society, George Hadden. When asked if an historical tour of Wexford town could be provided he blithely barked, 'Of course! Which century do you want?' To attempt a synopsis of this vast torrent of history and prehistory creates enough frustration to release an outraged bellow at one's own ignorance.

Wexford cannot be caged by any one race. It cannot be said to have been wholly Gaelic, Norse, Norman or Neolithic. Its position on the corner of Ireland next to mainland Europe, 50 miles from Wales and inside a placid safe harbour, was but one reason for its early eminence. Its nearby south and east coasts were the beachheads for numerous intruder landings. This strategic eminence was valid no less in our own time than in prehistory, as recently published Whermacht papers testify. However, when one seeks to unfold the shrouds surrounding Wexford's ancient community one is brought face to face with two factors. A town normally finds its origins in that it is the focal point of converging roads, routes or seaways. The first germ of Wexford's life stirred at the River Slaney ferry-crossing point, namely a huge rock now covered by the North Railway Station. The first market place was the present Cornmarket, near White's Hotel. Coinciding with these first stirrings we find also a place of religious significance — Christian, and certainly pre-Christian — overlooking the ferry-crossing. This is identified today as the ruins of Selskar Abbey. And further of significance but requiring much more study is the prehistoric religious relationship of the Island of Begerin to Selskar itself. For Begerin, now landlocked by reclamation, was the first island of known pre-Christian importance — the focal point of fear and worship of the Unknown which confronted any new intruder into Wexford Harbour. It too laid its hand on prehistoric and modern Wexford. Its long shadow is measured by the parish church of St Iberius, the successor of many previous churches, on the raised headland directly opposite the Sacred Island. St Ibar introduced Christianity to Begerin and Wexford before St Patrick's mission, but relative to Wexford's age that was only yesterday.

I cannot tell you who the first people were. I cannot suggest whether there were inhabitants when Britain and Ireland belonged to the European land mass, or whether they were colonists from overseas, part of the many pre-Gaelic colonisations. The Gaelic people, whose arrival is suggested to be not later than 350 BC, called the place Loc Garman. Physically it resembled a rounded 'W' with two water inlets, the deep pool at the Crescent Quay, the shallow one lapping up against the Cornmarket and modern White's Hotel. In between, on the high rock headland was erected inevitably the site of worship, today's St Iberius. At its southern end was its military strongpoint behind today's Talbot Hotel. This fortress on an unobtrusive controlling height of rock, with that absolute necessity, spring water in abundance, is still, after thousands of years, a military base.

The Norse influence

The Norsemen discovered the happy hunting ground in the seven hundreds. By 850 AD they were established in Loc Garman. They had taken the strongpoint and established their municipality, their places of worship and burial, at its base. They called their new base Weisfiord, the fiord of the flats. The political unit in which the Norsemen found themselves was known as Ui Ceinnselaig. It embraced all of modern counties Wexford and Carlow and south-west Wicklow. While the Norsemen strictly preserved their identity they ultimately paid fealty to the King of Ui Ceinnselaig and in time established trade, and mercenary links, whenever the need arose. From this period the

53

expansion of recognisable modern Wexford commenced. The streets in the old part of the town are still the same thoroughfares used 1110 years ago between the Norse settlement in the south and the Gaelic market township in the north around Cornmarket.

Keen students of licensed premises will have long noted the fact that between the Bullring and the site of St Peter's gate in Peter Street (known popularly as Gibson's lane) the public houses are all on the harbour side of Main Street. This emphasises another feature of Wexford. The streets are built on the original paths which ran between cliffs. Wexford's hidden rock outcrops makes her like the steps of an amphitheatre. Thus on the harbour side there was a drop and therefore cellar facilities. On the opposite side there was a sheet of rock behind the façades.

Almost three hundred years after their establishment the Norsemen sowed the seeds of their own expulsion with one hopelessly indiscreet gesture of contempt. In a complicated power struggle they and the Norsemen of Dublin sided against the King of Ui Ceinnselaig, Donncha MacMurrough. In the battle to decide the issue the King was slain and the Norsemen buried his body with a dog. Through a series of remarkable family mishaps this king was ultimately succeeded at the age of 16 by one of the major figures in Irish history, Dermot MacMurrough, who ruled for 41 years. In the closing years of that turbulent reign he hired reluctant mercenaries from Bristol and Wales with the promise of Norse Wexford as a fee, plus two cantreds of land to the south of it ('the land of the stranger people', and the sea disasters).

The Norman influence

In 1169 the Norman mercenaries replaced the Norsemen of Wexford. The new leader was Robert FitzStephen, the son of the Welsh princess Nesta, and the Constable of Cardigan. The idea current that these men arrived as unknown as Samurai must be eroded. Ui Ceinnselaig and Wexford were constituent and familiar parts of a maritime Irish Sea province, the communication between whose points was more easy and less hazardous by far than, say, communication with Connacht or Ulster. The exchange and use of mercenaries on both sides of the Irish sea was common.

The new owners of Wexford took control of the well-oiled machinery of a busy trading port painlessly. Business was

as usual. They fortified the Norse walls and placed turrets at the strategic points. They later extended the walls to surround the Gaelic township and the venerable site, Selskar Abbey.

With the Normans there commenced at Wexford a frenzy of ecclesiastical activity. The little churches which were sited outside the gates of the town were granted to the formidable order of the Knights Hospitalers of St John. This order had its first Irish headquarters – its Commendatory – at St John's Gate, the principal merchant entrance to the market place. They in turn granted the church outside St Mary's Gate to the new, and poor, order of St Francis. That was in 1242 and it is in this place that one can justly claim that the greater episodes of Wexford's church drama took place for the next 700 years in all their colour, misery, turbulence and intense missionary work. It was spared ultimate extinction later because of its position outside the walls. It is a remarkable coincidence that to this day all the churches in Wexford of all Christian traditions are sited near the town's medieval gates.

From medieval times to modern day

We have thorough records of the principal citizens of the medieval town but we can only surmise at the race and personnel which formed the infantry of Wexford. It was seafaring for the great part, in both deep and shallow waters. The seafaring and fishing families seemed to concentrate on the south side, with the Faythe as their personal enclave. The trade and merchant services claimed the rest. The mixture of races in Wexford coupled with its open door to the world gave Wexford, oddly, a cosmopolitan flavour. The street names of Constantinople, Bristol, Galatz and Cadiz were household names here in Wexford's days of sail.

Wexford had two phases of total war visited on it. By that I mean that it was not only a battlefield but it twice suffered phases of military liberation, overthrow and occupation, with each phase bringing its quota of atrocity, execution, revenge or outrage appropriate to the dominant cause. The first phase occurred during 'The Great Rebellion' or Confederate Wars 1641–1649 which concluded with Cromwell's sack of Wexford in 1649. The second phase took place in 1798 when all County Wexford was washed by an international power struggle and was provoked to blood and fire.

When the rebellion was over a generation of Wexford's people was mutilated irreversably in spirit, body and possessions. Wexford county lay in ashes. The provocations, the plans leading to this explosion, the overwhelming defeat of the revolt, launched everyone into a pit of numbing despair. In today's mind all other political and historical events are minor waves against the black granite mass of '98.

Modern times were kinder to Wexford. The 19th century saw an unprecedented era of prosperity. It was a time when the Wexford ship owner Devereux could boast a fleet of 99 ships. Wexford had its own ship building industry, became the centre of the Irish agricultural machinery industry, reclaimed 5000 acres from the harbour, and under the inspiration of the Redmonds reclaimed the north station and south station areas. The several wharfs were united and a new straight quayside introduced the seafront thoroughfare we have today. The continuing strategic importance of Wexford and its south-east corner was still stressed in the presence during the First World War of a submarine detection base, an airship base, an American seaplane base and a complementary battery of six-inch guns at Rosslare Harbour.

The Anglo-Irish War, the Civil War which followed, and the economic and political unrest of the thirties are of recent memory. Through all the vissisitudes the citizens on the Wexford concrete have never been bereft of a spirit of impertinent optimism. They have seen upheavals, revolutions, different rulers, awesome variety, even oppression because of chosen altar. The waves have come and gone. Yesterday's strangers are today's citizens; without any feeling that they should explain their presence. You know the names. They are Kinsella, Murphy, Kehoe, Doran, Nolan, O'Connor, Larkin, Doyle, Dake, Prendergast, Fleming, Sinnott, Roche, Walsh, Devereux, French, Lambert, Power, Neville, Rossiter, Furlong, Harvey, Miller, Hempenstall, Browne, Moore, Jenkins, Hamilton.

Wexford claims them all.

Left: *Wexford's narrow streets add to the sense of bustle and activity during Festival time.*

Above: *Ballyhack is one of many picturesque villages in County Wexford.*

THE MUSIC AT WEXFORD

'Michael William Balfe', by Wood.

M W Balfe: The Early Years

by T J Walsh

This important essay on the fascinating early career of Balfe appeared in the first Festival programme in 1951. It is typical of Dr Tom's erudition and already showed his capacity for detailed research and his far-ranging abilities as a music historian.

Michael William Balfe was born on 15 May 1808 at No. 10 Pitt Street, now Balfe Street, Dublin. His father, William Balfe, was a dancing master; his mother, Kate Ryan, was a relative of Leonard MacNally, counsellor, informer and author of the words of the song 'The Lass of Richmond Hill'. During the years 1814 and 1815, and probably for some years previous, Balfe senior spent from July to December in Wexford, teaching dancing and ending each season with an Annual Ball at the Assembly Rooms, where his pupils — 'young ladies' and 'young gentlemen' of the town and county — danced 'ballets, Tambourine and Castenet Dances, minuets, waltzes, hornpipes, reels, etc. etc'. Tickets cost five shillings each, the pupils began their performance at half past seven, and country dances commenced at ten o'clock.

A tradition exists that Michael William Balfe was taught to play the violin in Wexford during these periods, first by his father — whom, it is said, he used to assist at his dancing classes — then by a Joseph Halliday, the band master of the Cavan Militia, and finally by a Mr Meadows. It seems a reasonable surmise that Balfe's father was his first teacher, for the kit or pocket-sized violin was an indispensable item of the dancing master's profession, and being only some sixteen inches long, would make an admirable instrument for so young a child. That he was capable of playing for his father's dancing classes while only six or seven years old is borne out by his appearing as a solo violinist at the Theatre Royal, Crow Street, Dublin, on 25 June 1817, less than two years later, when *Saunders' News-Letter* reported: 'We really believe a more extraordinary exhibition of musical taste and talent in a child was never witnessed.'

In 1823, on the death of his father, he set out for London as an articled pupil of Charles Edward Horn, the composer and singer. In London he was engaged as a violinist in the orchestra of the Theatre Royal, Drury Lane, studied composition under C F Horn, the father of his teacher, and

appeared as Caspar in a garbled version of *Der Freischütz* at Norwich. In 1825 he found a patron in a Count Mazzara who took him to Italy, introducing him to Cherubini in Paris on the way.

In Italy he desultorily studied composition with Paer in Rome and with Vincenzo Federici at the Conservatoire in Milan. In Milan he also studied singing with the famous bass Filippo Galli, and for the Teatro alla Scala composed the music for a ballet, *La Pérouse.* He returned to Paris in 1827, where Rossini was *Inspecteur-Général du Chant de France.* On hearing him sing, Rossini advised him to take lessons from the famous singing teacher and tenor Bordogni, and promised to recommend him to the director of the Théâtre des Italiens. In January 1828 he made his debut singing Figaro in *Il Barbiere di Siviglia* with Sontag, Bordogni and Levasseur (Don Basilio), and shortly afterwards was given a contract for three years. During this engagement he sang roles such as Dandini in *La Cenerentola* (with Malibran, Donzelli and Zucchelli), Don Giovanni and the Podesta in *La Gazza Ladra.*

He also began to compose an opera, but he was obliged to curtail his engagement because of ill health — probably an early indication of pulmonary tuberculosis — and so he returned to Italy. During the Carnival Season of 1829–30 he sang at Palermo, making his debut as Valdeberg in Bellini's *La Straniera,* and here his first opera *I Rivali di se Stessi,* which he had written in twenty days, was produced. He sang next at Piacenza and then at Bergamo, where he met his future wife, the Hungarian soprano Lina Roser, then to Pavia to sing Pharaoh in *Mosè in Egitto,* but where instead he replaced the conductor. Here his second opera, *Un Avvertimento di Gelosi* was performed — a production distinguished only by the performance of the famous baritone Giorgio Ronconi, his second appearance on the operatic stage.

During 1834 a third opera, *Enrico Quarto al passo della Marno* was produced at La Scala, Milan. In a memorandum of his operas written out by Balfe almost fifty years later he gives the date of this production as 1831. This date has in turn been repeated in every treatise on Balfe for almost a hundred years, but the little evidence that exists seemed against it, and information obtained from the archives of La Scala confirms that the production did in fact take place in 1834. Later in the same year Balfe sang some roles at La Scala, possibly through the influence of Malibran, with whom he sang Iago in Rossini's *Otello*. On 26 March 1835, he commenced a season at the Teatro La Fenice, Venice, in a company headed by Malibran and the tenor Donzelli, singing his usual roles in *Otello, Il Barbiere di Siviglia* and *La Cenerentola*. On 3 April he appeared in *Il Barbiere di Siviglia,* and on 8 April at the Teatro San Giovanni Grisostomo, later named the Malibran in the diva's honour and now a cinema, he sang Count Rodolpho in *La Sonnambula*.

After the Venice engagement in 1835 Balfe was brought back to London by the Puzzis. The Puzzis were a colourful pair. Beginning in the 1820s, Signor Puzzi, an excellent horn player turned manager's agent, for thirty years brought virtually every important continental opera singer, and some equally unimportant, to London. But it was Madame Puzzi who was the personality, a second-rate soprano who became 'la Mamma degli Artisti'. Willert Beale speaks of her occupying her box on the third tier of Her Majesty's Theatre, almost hidden behind the yellow curtains, the passageway behind crowded with her friends. Here she would sit, encouraging some young artist shaking with stage fright on her first appearance, 'with a brava! that resounded through the house until it was echoed by the *flâneurs* in "fop's alley" and the stalls'. Through Signor Puzzi, Balfe first found engagements on the concert platform, and his career as a composer of English operas began with *The Siege of Rochelle*.

W J Lawrence has related how Balfe's debut as a singer in Ireland occurred not in his native Dublin but in Cork. Here on 28 July 1838, with a company that included the soprano Emma Romer and the tenor John Templeton, he commenced a season at the Theatre Royal, George's Street, as Count Rodolpho in *La Sonnambula*. Among the operas performed were his own *Maid of Artois* and *Diadeste,* and having left Cork the company visited Limerick. A review of Balfe's professional life in the year 1838 is of singular interest. His opera *Diadeste* came out at Drury Lane on 17 May, his *Falstaff* at Her Majesty's on 19 July. Nine days later he was appearing at Cork and then went on to Limerick. In October he was back at Drury Lane singing the Don in an English version of *Don Giovanni,* and finally on 10 November, after an absence of fifteen years, he returned to Dublin to begin a season at the Theatre Royal.

It is difficult to determine Balfe's true position as a singer. Too much importance should not be attached to his appearances at the Théâtre des Italiens and La Scala. Both his biographers, Barrett and Kenney, state that he was engaged in Paris as successor to Pellegrini, but Zucchelli, not Balfe, replaced Pellegrini at Paris, and there Balfe was a useful member of the ensemble rather than a star. It is also more than probable that his Scala engagement arose through the influence of Malibran, for in later years he was deeply fond of her. Willert Beale records that when the news reached London from Manchester of Malibran's death, Balfe, who was at his house, was completely overcome, and remained there for hours unable to control his grief. Beale also relates that 'his voice was not powerful and the quality was decidedly husky, but his style and his dramatic declamation of the simplest ballad were indescribably impressive'. Probably the best appraisal of his voice is to be had from R M Levey, sometime musical director at the Theatre Royal, Dublin, who heard Balfe sing there on many occasions. He relates 'Balfe did not possess a powerful voice but his vocalism was simply perfection. Bordogni was his singing master and it was indeed a treat to hear the pupil sing the elaborate and difficult arpeggios composed by the master for him'.

The fact that he was an outstanding musician and could read and memorise a score accurately and quickly, gave him a considerable advantage in Italy, where, early in the nineteenth century, *orecchianti* (singers who are incapable of, or have difficulty in, reading music) were infinitely more prevalent than they are today. Not that this was considered to be any great disadvantage to a singer's career. Stendhal observes 'that even a first rate singer did not necessarily have to know how to read music'. As viewed by an opera manager it had, however, two distinct advantages. Firstly, Balfe could learn a new role quickly and accurately, whereas the *orecchiante* required both time and a coach to learn the same role laboriously, and often very indifferently. Secondly, at a time when operas were composed in twenty days and rehearsed in four or less, a good musician on stage was of invaluable help to the other singers in the ensemble.

Balfe's first appearance on his return to Dublin in 1838 was as Count Rodolpho in an English version of *La Sonnambula.* The company was headed by Mrs Wood, *née* Mary Anne Paton, and her husband, both well known and popular artists in Dublin, who appeared as Amina and Elvino. On Monday, 12 November, *Saunders' News-Letter* declared: 'Equally earnest was the applause which greeted another individual, an Irishman distinguished by his talents as a composer and also known by report as a singer of very superior merit. We allude to Mr Balfe. He appeared as the Count Rodolpho and the manner in which he executed the first air at once established him a decided favourite. He is an admirable musician gifted with a baritone voice of the quality which falls with grateful impression on the ear and in the concerted pieces his assistance was found particularly valuable.'

All the operas were sung in English and on Monday, 12 November Balfe sang Dandini in Michael Rophino Lacy's version of Rossini's *La Cenerentola.* Again *Saunders' News-Letter* noted approvingly: 'With Mr Balfe the most fastidious ear could not find fault'. Lacy's version of Auber's *Fra Diavolo* was performed on the following evening without Balfe in the cast, but when the opera was over, a piano was pushed on to the stage and he sang 'The peace of the valley' and 'Travellers all of every station' from his operas *Joan of Arc* and *The Siege of Rochelle,* to his own accompaniment. On Wednesday he sang Eustace in Bickerstaff's ballad opera *Love in a Village,* introducing the airs 'Look forth my dearest' from *Catherine Grey* and 'The light of other days' from *The Maid of Artois,* and on Saturday Figaro in *The Barber of Seville.*

The second week of the season opened on Monday, 19 November with the ballad opera *Rob Roy MacGregor,* after which to his own accompaniment Balfe sang 'My Cottage near Rochelle' and 'Travellers all of every station'. On the following evening the forgotten ballad opera *Amilie or The Love Test* by the Irish composer W M Rooke (one of Balfe's early teachers) was played for the first time in Dublin. Rooke was born William Michael O'Rourke in Dublin in 1794 and in 1817 was chorus master and deputy leader at the Theatre Royal, Crow Street. In 1821 he crossed to England where he was subsequently well known at Drury Lane as chorus master, and at Vauxhall as leader under Sir Henry Bishop. Although his opera had been composed in 1818 it was not until December 1837 that it came out at Drury Lane, and this was its first performance in Dublin. The production created considerable interest, and to quote *Saunders' News-Letter,* 'it is scarcely necessary to observe that the distinguished merits of the composer were fully appreciated by his countrymen. The opera was brought out in a very creditable manner and several very pretty scenes were painted expressly for the occasion by Mr Phillips. The libretto, which is by a Mr Haines, is even worse than such things usually are. The plot in as far as it can be understood consists in the fact of a young girl Amilie (Mrs Wood) remaining faithful to her absent lover notwithstanding the persecutions of a rejected suitor Jose (Mr Wood) and ultimately her fidelity is rewarded by the return of her lover raised to a rank in the army by his bravery. Balfe in the role of General Count der Tiemer was enthusiastically applauded for his singing of the airs "What is the Spell?" and "My boyhood's home." ' The performance passed off with such success that the opera was given six times during the season.

For the next change of programme a version of Auber's *Masaniello* was performed on 30 November, after which Balfe sang his ballad 'They tell me thou'rt the favoured guest', words by Tom Moore, and an air from his opera *Diadeste,* and this arrangement of having Balfe sing some of his compositions to his own accompaniment on the evenings when he was not engaged in the operas continued to the end of the season.

On 8 December, in *The Maid of Judah* — Michael Rophino Lacy's *melange* of the Rossini pastiche, *Ivanhoe* — Balfe sang Cedric, but the principal production of the season was undoubtedly Beethoven's *Fidelio,* which took place on 15 December. The first English version of the opera had been performed at Covent Garden in 1835 with Malibran as Fidelio. In Dublin the cast was Fidelio, Mrs Wood; Florestan, Wood; Rocco, Balfe and Pizzaro, G Horncastle, a popular singing actor of the stock company. Miss Mamilton, another member of the stock company, sang Marcellina; the conductor was R M Levey. The word 'conductor' creates a misconception of Levey's correct role and title, which was 'Director and leader of the orchestra', for this was before the time of today's virtuoso conductor. Levey did in fact both direct and lead the orchestra; sitting on a very high seat he used his bow to conduct, play his violin, and not infrequently to silence interrupters with an admonitory wave at the upper gallery.

Fidelio created a profound impression, the music critic of *Saunders' News-Letter* unequivocally declaring

'*Fidelio* is one of the most charming productions we ever had the gratification of hearing. . . The opera has been produced in a superior manner to any we ever recollect and the instrumentalists upon whom so much depends played with admirable ability and steadiness. The orchestra was considerably increased on the occasion and all the performers evinced their anxiety to do justice to a work on which no amount of labour could be thrown away. Mrs Wood as Fidelio sang with great power and effect and from the character of the airs she was prevented (even if so disposed) from introducing any lavish ornaments. The magnificent aria 'Oh monster, whence proceeds the hate' was given with a dignity and expression suited to the composition and in the concerted pieces her voice peculiarly told. Mr Balfe also sang charmingly, and an exquisite duet between him and Mrs Wood, 'Pretending this', was encored. Mr Wood displayed considerable merit in the part assigned to him, and the opening song in the third act, which is remarkably difficult, arising among other causes from the nice gradations in it, was executed in a superior manner. The services of Mr Horncastle materially contributed to the pleasure of the evening, and it is but justice to remark that the choruses were effectively and correctly given. The chorus of prisoners elicited an enthusiastic encore. It was a touching production, and the little bit for the soprano voice commencing with the words 'To him who ruleth over' heightened the result arising from the whole. . . . The house was densely crowded and *Fidelio* was announced amidst loud plaudits for Tuesday Evening.'

A crowded audience again heard the opera on Tuesday, and once more the manager, Mr Calcraft, announced a repeat performance for the following evening 'amid loud and unanimous applause'. In fact the only critical comment to be found occurred in *Saunders' News-Letter* of 19

December, when it was hoped 'that the absurd military ballet will not be allowed to offend the public taste again in a classic opera'. *Fidelio* was performed three times, and for the last performance of the season Act III was played in a pastiche which included the last act of *La Sonnambula,* and the ballad opera *The Cabinet* with Balfe as Lorenzo, in which he sang 'Torn from all I love' from *Catherine Grey.*

Charles Lamb Kenney in his *A Memoir of Michael William Balfe* deduces that none of Balfe's operas was performed during this season because of a triangular dispute between Balfe, Mrs Wood and Miss Romer. Balfe was supposed to have promised to compose only for Miss Romer, whereupon Mrs Wood was supposed to have refused to sing in any of his operas. A far less devious explanation is at hand, however. Balfe joined the company at the last moment, after *Don Giovanni's* premature closure at Drury Lane, and Mrs Wood, although she had at least sung Isoline in *The Maid of Artois,* as the star of her company obviously saw no reason to change the repertoire simply to advance Balfe's career.

Balfe was the guest of honour at a dinner at Morrison's Hotel, Dawson Street, on 26 December. 'Several musical gentlemen were present', and John Barton, late leader of the orchestra at the Theatre Royal, Crow Street, and sometime violin teacher to Balfe, 'filled the chair'. On the head table were placed 'two very neat and tastefully executed Temples of Fame. On one of them the figure of Fame was raised bearing a banner with the name of the guest inscribed upon it. In the dome an Irish Harp with a chaplet of shamrocks enwreathed upon it. Upon the pedestal appeared the motto

Where'er I roam, whatever realms to see

My heart untravell'd fondly turns to thee.

The banners were inscribed with the names of the operas composed by Mr Balfe . . . the popular songs of Mr Balfe . . . were also noticed in an appropriate manner'. After dinner 'the musical gentlemen sang Neo Nobis Domine. The Chairman then gave in succession The Queen and the Lord Lieutenant. The National Anthem followed the first toast and Sir John Stevenson's Raise the Flag the second'.

During the evening Balfe made a speech and sang several of his own and Rooke's songs, and Calcraft, the manager of the Theatre Royal, who was among those present, promised Balfe's prompt return to Dublin in some of his own operas. Accompaniments for the singing were by harp, piano and guitar, and the company broke up about half past eleven. On the following day Balfe was presented at the hotel with a suitably inscribed testimonial gold snuff-box.

Balfe returned to Dublin ten months later when he opened a season at the Theatre Royal with his wife and the celebrated pianist Sigismond Thalberg. Two concerts were given on 14 and 15 October 1839, in which Balfe sang duets from operas by Donizetti, Rossini and Gabussi, and Madame Balfe sang 'Ah, non giunge' from *La Sonnambula.*

The regular winter season commenced on 19 October with *La Sonnambula.* John Templeton and Emma Romer from Drury Lane sang Elvino, and Amina and Balfe sang his old role of Count Rodolpho. On subsequent evenings he sang Figaro and Dandini, and on 24 October Mr Calcraft kept his word and presented Balfe in one of his own operas — *The Maid of Artois.*

When the opera was first produced at Drury Lane almost three and a half years previously, with Malibran as Isoline, it had had an immense success. *The Times* declared that 'the house was not only full before the opera commenced but was filled by a company whose appearance gave an *éclat* to the theatre that it does not always display'. Sixteen performances brought in an average of £355, while Macready in a season of Shakespeare could average only £189. Yet the notices were not all favourable. One critic commented that 'Bellini, Rossini, Meyerbeer, Weber and others might all claim their share in Balfe's achievement, but it was especially one waltz by Strauss of Vienna that won the new English opera loud and constant rolls of applause'. This was the *rondo-finale — The rapture swelling,* and its success was due entirely to Malibran. According to Sir Julius Benedict, 'nothing has ever exceeded the effect she produced in Balfe's *Maid of Artois,* the *finale* to which the *fioriture* with which it was embellished gave full scope to the phenomenal extent of her power of vocalisation'. According to Alfred Bunn, the librettist, she achieved all this by having a 'pot of porter' passed surreptitiously up through a small trap in the stage before she began her scene. The air became quite famous; (more famous than it deserved, one feels, hearing it now), so that some years later, when Balfe first visited St Petersburg, on being presented to the Empress Marie Feodorovna, she addressed him: *'Vous êtes Monsieur Balfe de l'air?'* Actually

the most popular air in the opera was the ballad 'The light of other days', and whereas Balfe's royalty from Drury Lane for the opera was five guineas a performance, the music sales of the ballad alone netted the publishers over six thousand pounds. Balfe wrote this ballad for the baritone role of the Marquis sung by Henry Phillips and did not produce it until the first orchestral rehearsal: ballads were always left until the last, the artists concentrating on concerted music and recitatives at the first rehearsals. On hearing Phillips sing it, and realising that it should create a sensation, Malibran as the star demanded it for herself, but Phillips held on.

Balfe next appeared as Doctor Dulcamara in *The Love Spell* — Donizetti's *L'Elisir d'Amore,* and on 7 November he appeared in his most famous opera at that time, *The Siege of Rochelle.*

This was first produced at the Theatre Royal, Drury Lane, on 28 October 1835, Balfe being announced as 'a native of Ireland who had been for some years pursuing his studies in Italy and was expected to remain in England, provided that encouragement was afforded, to which, on account of his talents, he was justly entitled'. The playbills described the production as a 'new grand original opera (founded on the celebrated novel by Madame de Genlis)'.

Balfe is said to have suggested the scenario himself, and later was accused of plagiarising part of the music from Luigi Ricci's opera *Chiara di Rosenberg.* This had been first performed at La Scala, Milan, in the autumn of 1831, and was soon being played all over Italy. Consequently it was likely that Balfe knew the opera. The list of roles in both operas is almost, if not entirely, identical, but one would need to examine both scores to form an accurate opinion of the charge, and the hearsay evidence available is entirely against it. *The Siege of Rochelle* was originally intended for Arnold's English Opera Company at the Lyceum, but through the interest of Balfe's old friend Tom Cooke it was eventually brought out by Alfred Bunn at Drury Lane. Balfe's royalty was again five guineas a performance and four hundred guineas from Cramer, Addison and Beale, the music publishers, for the copyright. It is noteworthy that English composers of the nineteenth century derived the major portion of their royalties not from stage performances of their operas but from music sales. When it is remembered that every Victorian drawingroom was a conservatoire for amateur singers — and every English lady and gentleman

63

of the period was expected to possess this accomplishment, it will be readily understood why the composers introduced so many effective, easily sung ballads into their works. The libretto was by Edward Fitzball and was 'somewhat weak' indeed, while the lyrics fully deserved J E Cox's opprobrium as being 'save the mark! – a degree below the style of the bellman's verses'.

Nevertheless the opera took London by storm. As Fitzball relates,

'It was a glorious night, the first night of *The Siege of Rochelle,* one to wish your whole life long the first night of a new play or a new opera. The cram there was, the fashion, the delicious music, the enthusiastic applause, the double encores, never had I witnessed anything like it. . . . The applause was so unanimous, so *really applause*. . . . So carried away were persons of even the highest consequence by the enthusiasm created by this beautiful music that people bent over and nearly threw themselves from the side boxes next to the orchestra to congratulate and shake hands with the young composer.'

The opera had a run of seventy performances. Queen Adelaide accepted the dedication of the work and had a set of silver bells made to accompany 'Lo, the early beam of morning', and when the young Queen Victoria paid her first state visit to the theatre after her accession, *The Siege of Rochelle* was performed 'by special desire'. In fact like Lord Byron after the publication of *Childe Harold,* overnight Balfe had found himself famous.

In Dublin the opera had been first performed by the stock company at the Theatre Royal on 14 May 1836, but the present production was a much improved one and Balfe's hand in it was evident. The cast was: Clara, Miss Romer; de Valmour, Templeton; Michel, Balfe and Montalban, Horncastle. Towards the close of the engagement, just before Christmas, there were some performances of Auber's *Fra Diavolo* in which Balfe appeared as Lord Allcash.

His next appearance at the Theatre Royal was in February 1840, in a company that included a Mr Franks, a Dublin tenor, Horncastle, and Madame Balfe as *prima donna.* Lina Roser had had a small career in Italy before she met and married Balfe. In 1832 we find her at Parma singing in Luigi

Ricci's unsuccessful opera *Il Nuovo Figaro.* The season in Dublin began on 13 February with *La Sonnambula* in which she appeared as Amina and was sharply criticised by the *Freeman's Journal.* Two days later, on 15 February, Balfe's opera, *Joan of Arc,* was performed with Madame Balfe as Joan, Franks as Theodore, Balfe as Badet and Horncastle as Renaud. The opera had been first produced at Drury Lane on 30 November 1837 with Fitzball again as librettist, and was a failure. The production in Dublin seems to have been reasonably successful, but the success was confined mainly to the ballad, 'The peace of the valley', sung by Balfe and, at the time, well known in Dublin from sheet music sales. *Saunders' News-Letter* of 17 February comments reassuringly: 'Joan is brought to the stake but the audience are saved the annoyance of an auto-da-fé. Just as the agony of the spectator is wound up to the highest pressure she is rescued and returns thanks for her salvation in a brilliant finale.'

On 25 February, by command of the Lord Lieutenant, Lord Ebrington, an English version of Luigi Ricci's *Scaramuccia* with Balfe as Tomaso, and Madame Balfe as Sandrina, was performed. The latter introduced an unpublished ballad of her husband's, called by one of the newspapers, for want of a title, 'Peace of Mind'. It was a successful and pleasantly impartial evening, cheers being given at the end of the performance for both Lord Ebrington and Daniel O'Connell.

On 7 March Madame Balfe took her benefit as Celina in Balfe's opera *Diadeste or the Veiled Lady.* The librettist was again Fitzball. It had been first produced at Drury Lane on 17 May 1838, announced as an *Opera-buffa,* but according to *The Musical World* 'for what reason we are at a loss to learn, for the music has not the slightest approximation to any comic school'. H F Chorley was even more ironic. In *The Athenaeum* of 19 May 1838 he wrote: 'The piece is (we understand) taken from the French, and we need no ghost to tell us that the music is taken from the Italian. The marks are partly taken out and the corners cut off in both instances but the proprietorship of the goods is distinctly traceable. There is nothing offensive in the music certainly, because there is nothing in it at all.' In fact the only successful feature of the production seems to have been some excellent sets depicting views of Venice painted by a famous family of London scene painters called Grieve.

In Dublin the opera had five performances, with Madame Balfe as Celina, Franks as Manfredi, Balfe as Count Steno and Horncastle as Zambo. This season was much less successful than Balfe's previous one; but then his company was much inferior, and half-filled houses were common.

Reading in retrospect of Balfe's status as a musician, one is immediatley conscious that he was a copyist, who almost, but never quite, attained the standard of a first class composer. H F Chorley, writing in 1862 of his opera *Falstaff*, which he had seen on its first performance in 1838, regretfully records it as being 'one of the many chances which this man of indisputable genius had been fortunate enough to obtain, I must add, willing to fling away'. He then goes on to say,

'There has been hardly a great singer in Europe since the year 1834, for whom he has not been called on to write; hardly a great and successful theatre in which his works have not been heard. He has the gift now rare, in late days, of melody, and a certain facile humour for the stage, which can hardly be overprized. His tunes are in our streets, but his best works cannot be said to last. . . With something of his own, there is something not so much of every country as of every composer in Mr Balfe's music. Here we meet an Italian rhythm, there a French interval, anon a German harmony, sometimes a strain of artless Irish melody. The listener most ready at identification would be puzzled to pronounce on the parentage of one of his English operas from the music itself, still more from those written by him to foreign text. This characteristic is too general among our composers who have written for the stage during the past five and twenty years. Perhaps it has been always so, as Arne's *Artaxerxes* (the one serious English opera which kept the stage) reminds us . . . other reasons for the ephemeral duration of Mr Balfe's operas may be cited: his disregard of character, accent and situation for the sake of catching effects and his peculiar taste in instrumentation. The latter, though sometimes effective, sometimes piquant, is too often thin; the stringed instruments are so carelessly grouped as to lose their nourishing sonority. . . The above may be so generally remarked as peculiarities in this fertile and successful composer's writings, that comment on them is no more indelicate than on the spasmodic climax of Signor Verdi, or on Mr Meyerbeer's particular habit of self-interruption. Owing to them it may be, that of *Falstaff,* only the animated trio of the two wives . . . and Anne Page . . . lives to tell the tale of Shakespeare's Merry Wives set in Italian for England by an Irishman and with such a French-Neapolitan artist [Luigi Lablache, whose mother was Irish] for its protagonist as would have made Shakespeare's heart leap for joy to look on.'

It is not coincidence that writing of his last opera *Il Talismano,* produced thirty-six years later, Sutherland Edwards has the same tale to tell. 'If in Balfe's last opera', he says, 'there is here something of Meyerbeer, there something of Verdi, there is also a great deal everywhere of Balfe himself.'

One could sum it up by calling him a first-rate eclectic. But Balfe was also a singer who composed for singers and, to quote Charles Santley, 'Nobody knew better than Balfe how to put music into a singer's throat'. As a man he seems to have possessed great charm. Perhaps nothing epitomises his character better than a simple letter written from St Petersburg on 6 March 1860, to E T Smith, the impresario.

Dear Mr Smith, I hear you have taken Her Majesty's Theatre; will you have me at my old post?* To save trouble and time I mention salary, £30 a week. I will work like a slave and be very useful as well as ornamental. A line here directed Poste Restante will find yours very truly, M W Balfe.

It is sad to have to relate that he was to be disappointed. Arditi and Benedict were engaged instead.

Balfe died of bronchitis at his home, Rowney Abbey in Hertfordshire, on 20 October 1870.

*As conductor.

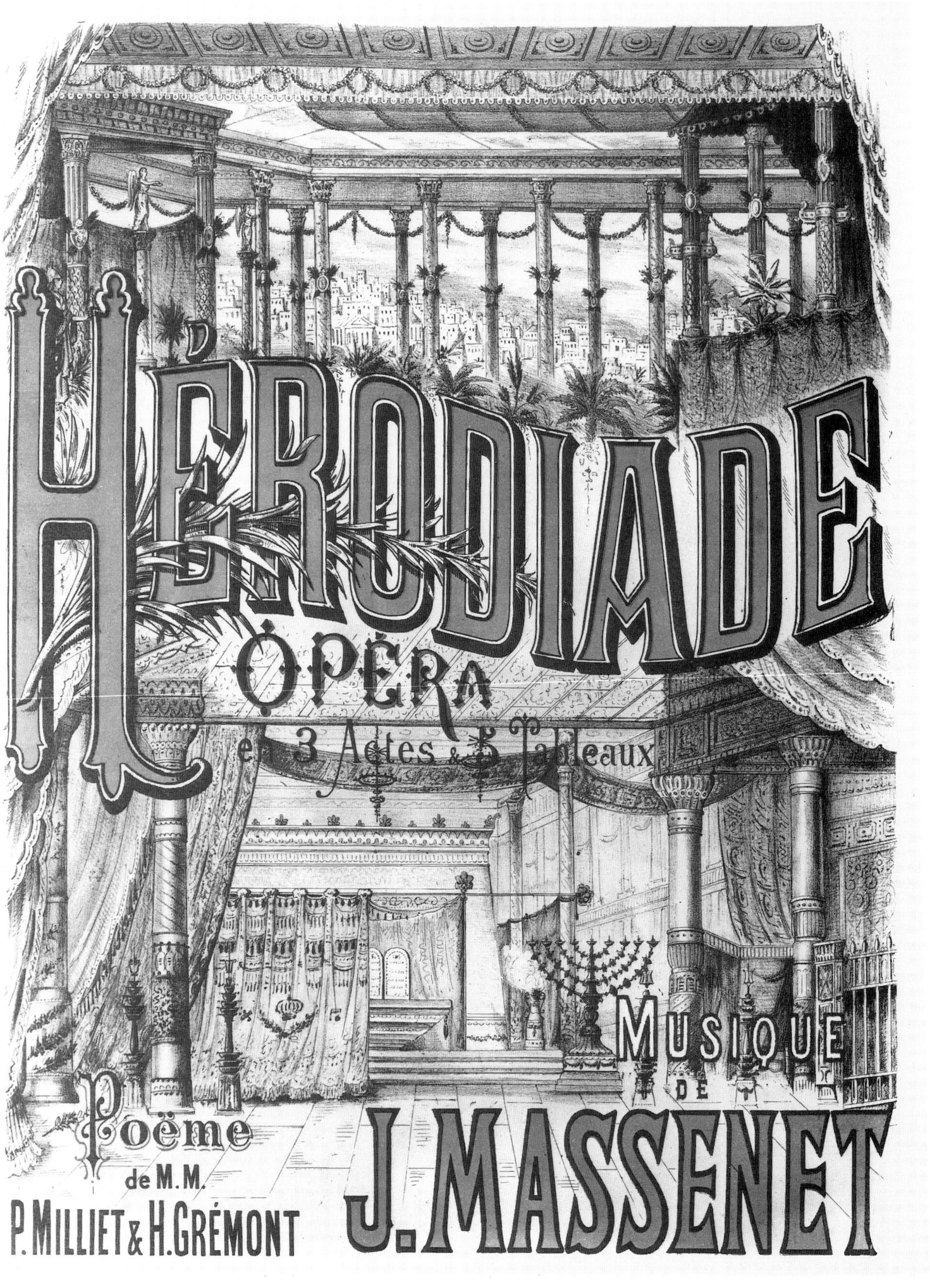
HÉRODIADE
OPÉRA
en 3 Actes & 5 Tableaux
Poëme
de M.M.
P. MILLIET & H. GRÉMONT
MUSIQUE
DE
J. MASSENET

The Libertine and the Statue

by Elizabeth Forbes

It would be churlish not to include Mozart in this anthology, 1991 being the 200th anniversary of his death. The Festival has provided a number of memorable productions of his less well-known operas, and also in 1988 another composer's view of his famous opera Don Giovanni. *In her article from that year* Elizabeth Forbes, *the distinguished London critic who is a long-standing visitor to and supporter of Wexford, traces the origins of the legend which led to the one-act version by Giuseppe Gazzaniga (1743-1818) which appeared in 1786, the year before Mozart's.*

The origins of legends are usually obscure. The legend of the Libertine and the Stone Guest who exacts retribution from him has roots buried deep in folk history; but the dramatic form of that legend has an easily traceable beginning, some four centuries ago in Madrid, with the birth of a male child. This boy, Gabriel Tellez, may have been the illegitimate son of Juan Tellez Giran, the Duke of Osuna and later the Spanish Viceroy in Sicily.

Tellez became a monk of the Mercedarian Order, taking his vows in 1601. For some years he lived in Toledo, where he made the acquaintance of Lope de Vega, at that period Spain's most popular dramatist and his senior by about twenty years. Under the name of Tirso de Molina, Gabriel Tellez also began to write for the theatre. His plays lack the brilliance, finish and style of the comedies of Lope de Vega; Tirso is rather slapdash in constructing his dramas, which read as if they were written in a great hurry; but he can draw characters, especially strong dynamic characters, with superlative skill, as Don Juan de Tenorio, the protagonist of his best-known play, *El Burlador de Sevilla y Convidado de Piedra,* eloquently demonstrates.

El Burlador (Tirso)

Don Juan springs to life with an energy, a fascination that leaps vividly across the centuries; he is not overshadowed by the innumerable other Don Juan characters since created by poets, playwrights, librettists and composers. Because he is the prototype, Tirso's Don Juan is worth examining in detail. The title of the play tells us that he is a trickster, a practical joker who finds the seduction of women the best joke of all. He is also a great impersonator, fond of dressing up in other men's personalities as well as their clothes. When lectured on his evil ways and asked when he is going to reform, he answers: 'There's plenty of time for that!'

The play opens at the court of Naples, where Don Juan has just seduced the Duchess Isabela, by the simple expedient of pretending to be her fiancé, the Duke Octavio. When his deception is discovered, he escapes by sea with his servant Catalinon. The two men are shipwrecked on the beach at Tarragona, where Don Juan seduces a beautiful and virtuous fisher girl, Tisbea, gaining her favours by promising to marry her. Abandoning Tisbea, he proceeds to Seville, where his father, Don Diego, is Chancellor to the King. In Seville Don Juan attempts to seduce Dona Ana, daughter of Don Gonzalo de Ullao, the Comendadore of Calatrava. He gains entrance to her room by impersonating the Marquis de la Mota, Ana's fiancé and one of his own closest friends. Dona Ana sees through the disguise and calls her father, who is killed by Don Juan as he escapes.

Feeling it prudent to leave Seville for a time, while his father tries to placate the King, Don Juan goes to Dos-Hermanas, where he is attracted by the peasant-girl Aminta and takes the place of her bridegroom Batricio on their wedding night. Back in Seville he visits the Cathedral and noticing the Statue of the Comendadore in a chapel, asks it to supper. The Statue accepts and that evening dines with Don Juan. On leaving, the Stone Guest asks his host back to supper in the chapel and Don Juan in his turn accepts. After a grisly meal of scorpions, vipers, vinegar and gall, Juan takes the Statue's hand and is instantly transported to hell. Meanwhile the Libertine's victims have converged on Seville, and after learning of his demise, they sort themselves out in couples, Isabela and Octavio, Ana and Mota, Aminta and Batricio. Only Tisbea is left without a husband.

Tirso's satire on the morals and behaviour of the Spanish aristocracy is quite withering. In the eyes of the Court, Don Juan's betrayal of his friend the Marquis is more dishonourable than his seductions of the women, which are condoned until the murder of Don Gonzalo. In 1625 Tirso was rebuked by his superiors for the frankness with which he represented vice in his plays, which deal with incest and blasphemy as well as murder and rape. For a while at least he appears to have given up the theatre. *El Burlador* was first published in 1930, but was certainly written and performed several years earlier than that. Tirso became Prior of the monastery at Soria and died in 1648, his place in dramatic history firmly established.

Don Juan, ou le festin de pierre (Molière)

The next major playwright to tackle the subject was Molière, whose *Don Juan, ou le festin de pierre* was first performed in Paris at the Palais-Royal on 15 February 1665, with the author himself in the rôle of Sganarelle, valet to Don Juan. Not surprisingly, Sganarelle plays a larger part in the drama than did Catalinon in *El Burlador.* Molière sets his play in Sicily, where Don Juan is escaping — or trying to escape — from the wrath of Donna Elvira, whom he deserted immediately after their 'marriage'. He plans to abduct his next victim, a young woman enjoying a seaside honeymoon with her lover, by boat. Unfortunately the boat sinks before Don Juan can achieve his purpose, but he is consoled by meeting two peasant girls, Mathurine and Charlotte, to each of whom he promises marriage. When the two girls meet, a tricky situation develops and Don Juan departs hastily with Sganarelle.

As they ride through the forest in disguise, Sganarelle tries to get his master to mend his ways. Is he not frightened of retribution for his misdeeds, in particular for the murder of the Commandeur six months before? Does he not believe in anything? Don Juan laughs. He believes that two and two make four, and that four and four make eight. After a meeting with two of Elvira's brothers, bent on revenging their sister's honour, Don Juan and his servant arrive at the tomb of the Commandeur, covered by a stone statue. Much against his will, Sganarelle is forced to ask the Statue to dinner. While waiting for his Stone Guest, Don Juan is

lectured by his father, Don Louis, and by Donna Elvira on the enormity of his behaviour. The Statue duly arrives and invites Don Juan to dine with him the following day. The Libertine pretends to repent, but the Statue returns and taking his hand, leads him down to hell for their dinner engagement.

The proliferation of the Don Juan theme

The first musical treatment of the Don Juan legend was composed by an Italian, Alessandro Melani. *L'Empio punito* (The Blasphemer punished), Melani's first opera, was performed in Rome in the presence of ex-Queen Cristina of Sweden in 1669. Henry Purcell provided incidental music (including the song 'Nymphs and Shepherds come away') for *The Libertine,* a play by Thomas Shadwell originally performed in 1676. Carlo Goldoni's tragicomedy, *Don Giovanni Tenorio, o sia Il Dissoluto,* was given during the carnival season of 1736 at the Teatro S. Samuele in Venice. In Vienna Gluck composed a ballet, *Don Juan, ou le Festin de Pierre,* based on Molière and performed at the Court Opera in 1761 — the year before *Orfeo ed Euridice.*

During the last quarter of the eighteenth century, operas on the Don Juan theme, many of them by Italian composers, tumbled over each other. In 1787 alone there were five different versions: the first of these was by Gazzaniga, the fifth by Mozart.

Don Giovanni Tenorio (Gazzaniga)

Giuseppe Gazzaniga was born in Verona in 1743. He studied in Venice, first with Porpora and then with Piccinni. His first opera, *Il Barone di Trocchia,* performed at Naples in 1768, scored quite a success. Two years later he wrote *Il finto cieco* (The false blind man) for the Court Theatre in Vienna; the librettist was none other than Lorenzo da Ponte. Gazzaniga's popularity was now assured. He received commissions for operas from theatres in Italy and other European countries. During the next thirty years he composed well over sixty operas and, after he became maestro di cappella at the Cathedral of Crema in 1791, much church music as well.

Don Giovanni Tenorio, o sia Il Convitato di pietro, his fiftieth opera, was first performed at the Teatro S. Moise in Venice on 5 February 1787. It was well received and before the end of the century had also been staged in

Bologna, Milan, Turin, Paris, Lisbon, London and Madrid. The text was by Giovanni Bertati, with whom Gazzaniga had first collaborated in 1771, on *Il Calandrino,* an opera given at the Teatro S. Samuele in Venice. Subsequently Bertati, whose best-known libretto today is *Il matrimonio segreto,* set by Cimarosa, provided Gazzaniga with many other texts.

Don Giovanni Tenorio had originally formed the second act (entitled *L'Italiano a Parigi*) of *La Novità,* set to music by F Alessandri in 1775; modified by Bertati, the complete text of *La Novità* became *Il capriccio drammatico,* with music by several composers; and finally the second act was readapted for *Don Giovanni Tenorio.* A copy of this text exists in the library of the Paris Opéra; on it, someone has scribbled: 'Written for the theatre S. Angelo in Venice. Spring 1782'. Were this true, it would place the first performance of Gazzaniga's opera five years earlier than is usually accepted, but no confirmation has been found. Perhaps the opera was intended for production in 1782 but Gazzaniga, who wrote two pieces for Palermo and one for the S. Samuele in Venice that year, did not have the time to compose it just then.

Gazzaniga's *Don Giovanni* is short, consisting of only five scenes. He introduces four female victims of Don Giovanni's lasciviousness: Donna Anna (from Tirso) in the first scene; Donna Elvira and the peasant girl Maturina (both from Molière) plus a new character, Donna Ximena, in the second and third. The last two scenes deal with the Stone Guest, his invitation to dine with Don Giovanni, his subsequent arrival, and the vengeance wreaked on the host. The opera ends with a sextet, in which the chief characters express their relief at the Libertine's demise by singing, dancing and imitating the instruments of the orchestra.

Don Giovanni (Mozart)

Meanwhile Wolfgang Amadeus Mozart, after the success of *Le nozze di Figaro* in Prague in 1786, had been commissioned to write another opera for the theatre in that city. Not surprisingly, after their joint triumph with *Figaro,* Mozart chose Lorenzo da Ponte as librettist. Da Ponte was already writing texts for two other composers – *L'arbore di Diana* for Vicente Martin y Soler, and an Italian adaptation of *Tarare* for Antonio Salieri – and it was no doubt lack of time that made him crib so shamelessly from

Bertati's text when he came to write *Il dissoluto punito, o sia Don Giovanni* (as it was originally titled) for Mozart. Da Ponte lifted the first two scenes of *Don Giovanni Tenorio* almost unchanged in form, sometimes making use of Bertati's very words (in Leporello's Catalogue aria, for instance, which closely resembles the duet for Pasquariello and Elvira in Gazzaniga's opera). Da Ponte ignores Bertati's third scene, which deals mainly with the quarrel that breaks out between Donna Elvira and Maturina, and his text is then his own work until the cemetery and supper scenes, which correspond to Bertati's scenes 4 and 5. Plagiarism was not considered a crime in those days.

Mozart's *Don Giovanni* was first performed in Prague on 29 October 1787; six months later it was produced in Vienna; it reached London in 1817 and soon became one of the most popular and greatly admired operas ever written. After its initial success, Gazzaniga's *Don Giovanni* – indeed all his stage works – was forgotten. But poets, dramatists and composers continued to find inspiration in the theme. E T A Hoffmann wrote a brilliant story on the subject; Byron's unfinished epic poem *Don Juan* scandalised half Europe; of the many operatic versions composed in the nineteenth century, Dargomyzhsky's *The Stone Guest,* posthumously performed in 1872, is the most memorable. Dargomyzhsky chose one of Pushkin's *Little Tragedies* (written in 1830) as his text, setting the verse unaltered. In this version the man killed by Don Juan, whose statue he later invites to dinner, is Anna's husband, not her father. Anna is on the point of succumbing to Juan – she did not love her husband, an older man chosen by her parents – when the Stone Guest arrives to safeguard her virtue.

The legend continues . . .

In the twentieth century, writers have been even more free with the legend. In *Don Juan in Hell,* the central episode of G B Shaw's play *Man and Superman,* Juan is seen in flight from Anna, who represents the Life Force. He complains that women have always pursued him, not the other way round. The legend has come full circle. Tirso de Molina, Molière and Mozart are the giants who tower above all other contributors to the Don Juan dramatic literature, but Gazzaniga will not be forgotten – da Ponte's borrowings from Bertati ensure his immortality.

The original Don Giovanni

by T J Walsh

In 1952 the Wexford Festival published a fascinating book by its director, entitled Opera in Old Dublin 1819-1838. *In it* Dr Tom *traced the story of operatic productions of the period, devoting Chapter One to the first presentation of Mozart's opera* Don Giovanni *in Ireland. It is of special interest not only because of the Mozart bicentenary, but also because it is his first historical study, which was to lead much later to his important studies on opera in Ireland and France. His comment on Mayr is particularly interesting, with that composer's* Medea in Corinto *appearing at the Festival in 1974.*

On the morning of Monday, 27 September 1819, an advertisement in the Dublin daily papers, respectfully informed the public that the Theatre Royal, Crow Street, would re-open that night with 'Mozart's celebrated opera of *Il Don Giovanni* as performed three seasons with the most rapturous applause at the King's Theatre, London, by the following principal performers from the said Theatre: Signora Corri, Signora Mori, Miss R Corri, Signor Begrez, Signor Romero, Signor Deville and Signor Ambrogetti — the original Don Giovanni.'

Readers were also informed that the leader of the band would be 'Mr Mori (Leader of the Philharmonic Society of London),' who would 'perform grand solo concerto on the violin between the acts,' that Mr Corri would be 'the conductor of the pianoforte,' and that 'the additions to the band would be more numerous than on any previous occasion.'

The birth of Italian opera in Ireland

Italian opera had been introduced into Ireland in March, 1711, when a company headed by the renowned eighteenth-century singer, Nicolini, performed Handel's *Rinaldo* at the Smock Alley Theatre, Dublin. There is some evidence that the company was formed by the Irish impresario, Owen MacSwiney, who was then part lessee of the King's Theatre, London, for MacSwiney had signed an agreement with Nicolini at this time.

A second opera performed during this engagement was M A Bononcini's *Il Trionfo di Camilla Regina de Volsci.* In 1761 two Neapolitans, Tommaso Giordani, a musician,

and his brother Francesco, a dancer, commenced another season of Italian opera at Smock Alley, Scolari's *La Cascina* being one of the operas produced.

Tommaso eventually married and settled down in Dublin, where he taught the piano, Lady Morgan being one of his pupils. About 1778, in partnership with the famous Jewish tenor Leoni, he opened the Little Theatre in Capel Street where they produced English opera. He was there joined by a third brother, Giuseppe, still remembered for his song, *Caro mio ben.*

During the winter of 1776-77, Anfossi's *Il Gelosa in Cimento,* Piccinni's *La Buona Figliuola* and Paesiello's *La Frascatana* were performed at Smock Alley. Of these *La Buona Figliuola,* or to give it its full title, *La Cecchina ossia le buona figliuola,* of Piccinni, only, requires comment. First produced at Rome in 1760, the libretto by Goldoni, based on Samuel Richardson's *Pamela or Virtue Rewarded,* it in time became probably the most popular *opera buffa* ever composed. *La Cecchina* in fact became the rage of Italy — shops, villas, wines and fashions being named after her.

The season was a failure, however, the artists, with the exception of the buffo singer Sestini, being inadequate, the house usually empty and miserably cold. Ultimately, the impresario, a Portuguese with the euphonious but bogus title of Il Cavaliero Don Pedro Martini, although enjoying the patronage of a number of the nobility, including the Duke of Leinster, found he was unable to pay his company, who promptly dispersed. The subsequently famous Irish tenor, Michael Kelly, made his debut during this season, taking the place of a Signor Savoy who had fallen ill, and singing the part of The Count in the first performance of

La Buona Figliuola. The prices of admission were: Boxes and Pit, half a guinea; First Gallery, five shillings; Upper Gallery, three shillings. Bags and swords were then the order of the day, and etiquette demanded that the orchestra as well as the audience in the boxes and pit should wear evening dress.

Don Giovanni reaches Dublin

The present performance of *Don Giovanni* – thirty years after its production in Prague, and two after its first authentic London performance – was the first presentation of a Mozart opera in Dublin, and we learn that a number of amateurs who had attended a rehearsal on the previous evening were favourably impressed.

Conversely the professional critics hardly noticed the season, and have left almost nothing but a few lines concerning the first performance of *Don Giovanni* of which, we are informed, 'many are applying for the Box Sheet, among whom are persons of leading rank and fashion and great respectability.' This lack of interest may have been due to the low ebb at which the fortunes of the Crow Street Theatre then were, and we read of the Italian Opera Company having arrived in town, whereupon it is presumed that the Theatre would reopen – as if it were thought highly likely that it might not.

The prices of admission were: Boxes, 5/5; Pit, 3/3; Galleries, 2/2, but although the performance was 'admirably well got up', the theatre was poorly attended.

Don Giovanni was again presented on Wednesday evening, and on Thursday, Mayr's opera buffa *Il Fanatico per la Musica* was performed. This opera and its composer are now forgotten, although both were once very popular. Simon Mayr was Donizetti's teacher. He is said to have introduced the crescendo into opera, which was later so effectively employed by the eclectic Rossini, the popularity of whose comic operas in turn forced the operas of Mayr off the stage. As the name implies, *Il Fanatico* concerns the eccentricities of one Don Febeo. Included in the opera is a rehearsal scene, of the type extremely popular with buffo bassos at this period. Fioravanti introduced one into his *Le Cantatrici Vilane,* Paer one into *Le Maître de Chapelle.* Today the scene which would perhaps most closely approach it is Danny Kaye conducting the chorus in *The Inspector General.*

On Saturday there was a grand dramatic selection consisting of the overture and quintette *Hm! Hm! Hm!* from *Il Flauto Magico,* quintette from *Cosi fan tutte,* the finale of *Il Barbiere di Siviglia,* and arias and duets by Bishop and some forgotten composers, the performance ending with a repetition of *Il Fanatico per la Musica.*

On Thursday, 7 October, 'the comic opera (never acted here) of *Figaro',* was performed, and on Saturday this was repeated under its more correct title of *The Marriage of Figaro.*

It is possible that the operas were cut, as it is evident from the advertisement that there were insufficient artistes in the company to complete the cast for *Le Nozze di Figaro* unless some of the smaller parts were sung by members of the theatre's stock company. The parts of Masetto and the Commandant in *Don Giovanni* were presumably doubled.

Of the singers engaged, Begrez (tenor), De Ville (basso cantante), Romero (basso), and Signora Mori (soprano, and sister of the violinist) were all secondary singers from the King's Theatre, London. In a season extending over five months there, where a star like Camporese would be paid a fee of £1,650, they received £400, £300, £410, and £300 respectively.

The Corri family

The Corri family was later to become closely identified with the musical life of Dublin. The original Corri was one Domenico, an ephemeral composer and pupil of Porpora, who was born in Rome in 1746. In 1771 he came to Edinburgh, where he had three sons. Of these, Haydn, the youngest, born in 1785 and christened after the famous composer, seems to have been the cleverest, and is the only one that concerns us.

He began life by winning distinction as a boy vocalist, and later trained the celebrated Madame Vestris for her debut in opera. In 1815 he married Miss Anna Adami, a young singer attached to the Theatre Royal, Covent Garden, who is the Signora Corri mentioned in the advertisement. In 1821 Henry Harris, having built the first Theatre Royal in Hawkins Street, Dublin, engaged Mrs Corri as the second soprano in the inaugural stock company.

She seems to have been both popular and competent, though not very accomplished as an actress, for in the

71

Theatrical Observer we read that 'Mrs Haydn Corri, as Julia Mannering [in *Guy Mannering*] gave us her usual number of dodgings to the right and to the left'.

With the debut of his wife at the new Theatre Royal, Haydn Corri, believing that there was an opening for his talents in Dublin, decided to make his home there. Already known as a pianist and conductor, and as the composer of a few glees and songs, he set up at No. 25 Bachelor's Walk as a teacher of singing and the piano. He was subsequently appointed organist to the Pro-Cathedral in Marlborough Street, a position which he held for thirty-five years. He died at the age of 75 at No. 13 Queen's Square, on February 19, 1850.

Miss R (osalie) Corri was a first cousin of Haydn Corri.

Nicholas Mori, the leader of the orchestra, was reputed to have been 'one of the most shining ornaments of the great school of Viotti' but the same critic deplores the lack of finish in his playing, and his lack of taste in heading his programme for a benefit concert, with the design of a skull and crossbones, and the motto *Momento Mori*!

Giuseppe Ambrogetti

The outstanding member of the company was unquestionably Giuseppe Ambrogetti. He was a baritone, in his day so famous that it is difficult to understand the meagre references to be found concerning him in contemporary books and newspaper articles on singers and opera. He was born in 1780, and is said to have sung in Paris in 1815. William Ayrton, musical director at the King's Theatre, engaged him in 1817 for the first authentic London performance of *Don Giovanni*. His salary for a season at this theatre being £600.

Vocally, he seems to have been no better than average; — Lord Mount Edgcumbe refers to his 'want of voice and deficiency as a singer,' — but all contemporary authorities are agreed that he was an actor of exceptional ability. He appears to have excelled in two rôles, *Don Giovanni* and the mad father in Paer's *Agnese,* an opera based on Mrs Amelia Opie's novel, *Father and Daughter.*

George Hogarth tells us that while learning the latter rôle 'he had studied the various forms of insanity in the cells of Bedlam, but unfortunately in seeking to make his representations true, he made it too dreadful to be borne. Females actually fainted, while others endeavoured to escape from so appalling a picture.'

Writing in 1872, J E Cox says of his performance as the Don: 'With the exception of Garcia there has not since been such a representative, either at home or abroad.'

All this approbation is endorsed by his performance in Dublin. His acting in *Il Fanatico* is described by the *Freeman's Journal* as a 'masterpiece'. Of his *Don Giovanni,* the same writer relates: 'Independent of the singing it was as complete a piece of acting in that line, as we can remember to have seen, we know not which to admire most, the graceful easiness of his deportment, or the arch gaiety of expression which he threw into his features. He was rapturously encored in the *La ci darem la mano,* and was greeted with frequent bursts of applause during the evening. His voice does not possess much compass, but he supplies the deficiency by the exquisiteness of his taste. In the last scene when surrounded by fiends, the vehemence of his actions, his exclamations, and his appropriate attitudes, confirmed him in our opinion as an accomplished actor.'

The reference to 'fiends' makes this a suitable place to introduce, or rather refute, an extraordinary legend concerning Ambrogetti. Almost all contemporary references relate that towards the end of his life he entered the monastery of La Grande Trappe, where becoming a monk, he eventually died.

Messrs Levey and O'Rorke in *The Annals of the Theatre Royal, Dublin,* add verisimilitude to the story by announcing that this was due to his seeing one more than the attested number of six fiends among the chorus each evening in the last scene of *Don Giovanni* during the Dublin performances.

In fact, the only writer to rebut the fallacy is John Ebers, who states that 'after a temporary retirement (which gave rise to a report of his having embraced a religious life), he appeared again as a singer and, I believe, with renewed powers.'

An old play bill, dated 18 May 1822, advertising a concert at Drury Lane in which he took part; — oddly enough 'in aid of the Fund, now raising for the immediate assistance of the Extreme Temporary Distress of Several Provinces or Districts of Ireland' — seemed to support Ebers' story, and information from the Abbey of La Grande Trappe, and from Mount Melleray Abbey, where a contributor to Grove's

Dictionary of Music and Musicians, had him join the reformed Cistercians in 1833, placed it beyond doubt.

Perhaps Ebers also unwittingly indicates the source of the fallacy when he adds: 'With an overwhelming humour the outgushings of which never failed in its effect on others, Ambrogetti was himself the most wretched of men, a prey to horrors of hypochondria.' To modern perception this reads remarkably like recurrent melancholia, when he would probably forsake the stage and even seclude himself from his friends until the attack had passed. It is even conceivable that during an attack he might have sought admittance to the Cistercian Order of La Trappe, but not being accepted had left the Monastery after a time there.

On the afternoon of Sunday, 10 October, Signors Begrez, Romero, Ambrogetti and Mori joined with a number of Dublin artists to give a 'grand concert of vocal and instrumental music' at St Michael and St John's Church, in Exchange Street, 'for liquidating the debts incurred for building the organ and improving the chapel'. (The church stands on ground originally occupied by the Smock Alley Theatre.)

Tickets were five shillings each, and items principally by Haydn, and some forgotten eighteenth-century composers, were performed, the concert ending with the *Hallelujah* chorus from Beethoven's *Mount of Olives* sung by the choir.

On Tuesday, 12 October, the Italians gave a final performance of *Don Giovanni,* and the engagement ended. It was the first season of Italian opera still remaining in the repertoire to be given in Dublin. Ten years were to elapse before Italian opera was heard there again.

The Ricci brothers and the end of opera buffa

by Patric Schmid

Patric Schmid's *research has led to the resurrection of many neglected nineteenth-century operas. He has collaborated with Wexford on the preparation of a number of notable revivals, in particular the rediscovery of the Ricci brothers, whose one-act opera* La Serva e L'Ussero *(1977) featuring Sesto Bruscantini, whetted appetites sufficiently for the Festival to undertake the full-length comedy* Crispino e la Comare *two years later. As artistic director of Opera Rara, he has also produced a memorable series of recordings of outstanding productions of neglected operas, including the 1991 Donizetti selection,* L'Assedio di Calais.

In 1829 Rossini had laid down his pen. Donizetti had died in 1848. No more Italian Girls or Barbers. No more Don Pasquales or L'Elisirs. Opera buffa was dead.

But before it could be buried, it was to give one last joyous shudder — *Crispino e la Comare*.

It was the fourth and last collaboration of the Ricci brothers, Luigi and Federico. Luigi, the elder by four years, was born in Naples in 1805, and at the age of nine he had entered the conservatory of S. Pietro a Majella to study the violin. Four years later he was joined there by Federico. The brothers were inseparable and were soon known as 'the Siamese twins'. In temperament, however, they were like two sides of the same coin. Luigi was ebullient, witty and good-humoured; Federico was shy, self-effacing and tongue-tied in the company of the other pupils — who included Mercadante and the young Bellini.

Zingarelli — a noted composer at the end of the 18th century, and now considered the greatest teacher in the Kingdom of the Two Sicilies — had high hopes for Luigi, as a composer of church music. His hopes were quickly dashed. Luigi's metier was opera buffa, and between 1823 and 1827 he turned out a string of comic works that had Neapolitan audiences hailing him as the heir to Rossini's throne. But like Rossini, he yearned for the acclaim that was only awarded to serious composers. An acclaim he finally received, after a succession of near-hits and misses, with *Chiara di Rosembergh* at La Scala in 1831. Having proved he could write an acceptable serious work, he turned back to comedy, and in 1835 he was invited to provide a vehicle for Maria Malibran, *Il Colonello,* for the Teatro Fondo in Naples.

Federico, in the meantime, had completed his studies and was ekeing out a meagre living directing sacred music in the churches and cathedrals of the city.

Luigi now suggested they collaborate on *Il Colonello*. (Malibran did not, however, sing the brothers' work. On a carriage ride through Naples a pig had run between the horses' feet and her carriage had overturned. Bravely, Malibran had sung performances of *La Sonnambula* with her arm in a sling, but declined to take on the rigorous task of performing a new work. Instead, the heroine was sung by Carolina Ungher, remembered today as being the soloist in the first performance of Beethoven's Ninth who had turned the deaf composer around to see his applause).

Il Colonello was a great success, and the brothers collaborated again the following year at the same theatre with *Il Disertore per Amore*.

This second success did not inspire further collaboration, however. The brothers went their separate ways, Federico to make his own with operas as famous in their time as they are forgotten today, *La Prigione d'Edimburgo* and *Corrado d'Altamura,* while Luigi became maestro di cappella of the cathedral and director of the opera house in Trieste.

It was ten years before the brothers once again wrote an opera together; *L'Amante di Richiamo* for the Teatro d'Angennes in Turin. It was coldly received, and the brothers separated again.

In the ten years that had passed their personalities had undergone a drastic change. Now it was Federico who was witty, self-assured, confident, lionised, while Luigi had become morose, unsure and unable to recapture the success

Luigi Ricci

he had achieved with the still-popular *Chiara di Rosembergh* and *Un'Avventura di Scaramuccia.*

Nevertheless, it was Luigi who was invited by the impresario of the Teatro San Benedetto in Venice to provide a comic work for the Quaresima season of 1850. Luigi agreed — if Federico would once more collaborate.

The venture did not bode well. The work was to be based on an 18th-century Neapolitan farce with the unfarcical title of *Death and the Cobbler Doctor,* and the libretto was to be written by Piave — best known for his humourless melodramas for Verdi — *Il Corsaro, Ernani, I due Foscari.*

It was not even to be called an opera buffa. Piave had titled his libretto a melodramma fantastico-giocoso.

For all that, on 28 February 1850 the Venetian audience stayed long after the curtain had come down to cheer a comic masterpiece that held the operatic stage around the world until early in the 20th century.

Piave had provided the brothers with something new in comic opera, by going back to the very roots of the genre — satire. His text was a merciless dig at the medical profession. 'But how can I be a doctor?' asks Crispino of the Fairy who has just promised to elevate him from the role of humble shoe-maker, 'I'm only an idiot.' 'You'll be undetectable from a hundred others,' she replies sourly. The Hippocratical Latin Piave invents for Crispino's prescription is as pertinent to audiences today as it was to audiences of 125 years ago — 'Panem, salamen, e quattro broccoletti' . . . 'bread, salami and four brussels sprouts.' And what other librettist of the time would have dared to make people laugh at an attempted suicide and the on-stage death of one of his leading characters, the miser, Don Asdrubale!

Inspired perhaps by Piave's novel libretto, the brothers dressed it in the most enchanting music they had ever written. Bravura waltzes, sparkling ensembles, breakneck duets and trios.

If *Crispino e la Comare* was the last opera buffa, then it was also the first of a new kind of comic opera that would come into its own that same decade in Paris, at the hands of Offenbach. It seems apt that one of Federico's last successes should be on those same boulevards at the height of Offenbach's fame, when he revised *Crispino* for the French stage as *Le Docteur Crispin,* with the addition of several musical pieces for the secondary characters of Lisetta and Contino.

The first edition of the vocal score of *Crispino* was dedicated by the brothers to the Contessa Matilde Berchtoldt-Strachan. Their dedication was never explained, but one cannot help wondering if it was the Countess who figured in one of Federico's favourite stories. He delighted in telling his friends of the afternoon when he answered a knock at his door to find a negro servant on the step. 'My mistress, the Countess, has sent me to study with you,' the servant told him nervously. Unwilling to offend a patroness, but unsure just how much knowledge he could impart to a middle-aged servant, he asked, 'and if I accept you as a pupil, for how long are you to study with me?' 'I have to be back in time to prepare the evening meal,' was the answer. 'But I can't teach you to compose an opera in four hours!' said the startled Federico. 'Compose an opera?' said the confused servant. 'The Countess has sent me to learn how you cook macaroni!'

The brothers were never to write an opera together again. Federico became the director of the St Petersburg opera and, ironically, nine years after *Crispino* was born, Luigi died, surrounded by the doctors he had mocked, in an insane asylum in Prague. By the time Federico died in 1877, the works of both brothers had long since disappeared from the stage. Only *Crispino* survived . . . and far longer than many of the Rossini comic operas in the repertoire today. It was still being performed in New York in 1919, and in Turin as late as 1937. It was given a new lease of life in the 1950s when it was revived by Italian radio for Graziella Sciutti and again, with enormous success, in 1978. In England, Opera Rara performed excerpts from the opera in London, in 1970, and at the Bath and Hintlesham Festivals in 1971 and 1973, and it returned to Covent Garden after 80 years absence when the Act 1 finale was sung by Margreta Elkins and Tom McDonnell in 1975. Annetta's aria 'Io sono non piu l'Annetta' is a favourite Joan Sutherland encore and is also included in her 'Command Performance' album on Decca records.

Opera buffa may be dead, but long live *Crispino e la Comare*!

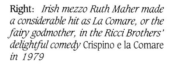

Above: *The great Italian buffo Sesto Bruscantini starred in the 1977 triple bill which introduced the Ricci Brothers' music to Wexford. He is seen here in his solo* tour-de-force, Il Maestro di Capella *(Cimarosa).*

Right: *Irish mezzo Ruth Maher made a considerable hit as La Comare, or the fairy godmother, in the Ricci Brothers' delightful comedy* Crispino e la Comare *in 1979*

Leoš Janáček

An introduction and historical note by Brian Large

Brian Large *studied music in London before moving to Vienna, where he wrote definitive books on the music of Smetana and Martinů. He is best known today as the world's leading TV director for opera, with such award-winning features as* The Three Tenors, *the Bayreuth* Ring *and the Met* Aida. *He was appointed a Fellow of the Royal Academy of Music in 1991. He contributed a valuable study of Janáček to the 1972 programme, the year that* Katá Kabanová *was produced at the Festival.*

Janáček was a revolutionary. His life was rich and spanned seventy-four years, during which he was a teacher, historian, lecturer, conductor, author, critic, ethnographist, founder and director of the Brno Organ School and professor of composition in the Brno Conservatoire. He was also one of the most original and significant personalities in Czech music and quite unlike his contemporaries. He was only thirteen years younger than Dvořák and should by all logic have belonged to the music of the nineteenth century, yet the reverse is true. His character, conception of art and musical expression were distinctly his own. He was a dramatist and for him life was one huge drama.

He was born in 1854 in Hukvaldy in Eastern Moravia in a rugged border region known as Lachia, and spent the first ten years of his life in an atmosphere of homely music making. His father, the local teacher, also trained the Hukvaldy Church Choir, but it was to the choir of the Augustinian Monastery in Brno that Leŏs was sent, where for the next seven years Pavel Krízkovsky (one of his father's pupils) was his mentor. Janáček's thirst for musical knowledge led him to the Prague Organ School where, between 1874 and 1876, he was coached as a singer, pianist and organist. Later he went to Leipzig and Vienna in the hope that he would establish himself, but doomed to disappointment he returned to Brno, taking up a teaching post in the local Training College in 1880. Here he began to compose, but spent a good deal of his time in the company of Frantisek Bartos, an enthusiastic collector of folk music, with whom Janáček edited, harmonised and performed collections of Moravian folk songs. At this time Janáček became obsessed with the idea of folk art. He lived in a world filled with the echoes of folk idiom and published a lengthy treatise on the characteristics of Moravian folk song. Later he organised festivals of Moravian folk art and ethnographic exhibitions in Prague; but most lasting was his work in founding the Brno Organ School, an institution set up in 1881 to train Moravian composers. He became the School's director and remained its unflagging organiser until 1919.

Janáček, the composer

In 1890 he began to devote himself more seriously to composition. Cantatas such as *Amarus* and *The Lord's Prayer* appeared alongside *Lachian Dances* for orchestra, the *Suite for Strings* and various part-songs for male voices; but most of his energy was devoted to an opera (his second) called *The Beginning of a Romance* which confirmed the composer's natural dramatic talent hinted at in *Sárka* (original version 1887) his first attempt at opera. But whereas *Sárka* is a heroic, mythological theatre piece and *The Beginning of a Romance* a series of tableaux with arias, in *Jenufa* (1894-1903), his third opera, Janáček's overall concept of opera altered. Here he produced a realistic music drama with a plot woven out of the conflicts, crises and jealous entanglements of the inhabitants of a small village community. Here he reproduced real, live drama on the stage with a power and musical force quite new to Moravian, or even Bohemian music at that time. Though *Jenufa* was premiered in Brno in 1904, twelve years were to elapse before it was given in Prague. During this period Janáček completed *Fate,* an opera in three Acts with much fine music but a notoriously weak libretto, and sketched the satirical *Excursions of Mr Broucek* who, under the influence of 'one too many' finds himself first on the moon and later in Prague of the fifteenth century. But before

Broucek was finished *Jenufa* was at last heard in Prague. The year was 1916 and the event was one for which Janáček had striven for at least ten years. The tremendous success Prague accorded *Jenufa* gave the sixty-two-year-old and virtually unrecognised composer a new surge of vitality; and when in 1918 Bohemia, Moravia and Slovakia were united to form the independent Republic of Czechoslovakia, Janáček was driven into a state of feverish activity for which at the age of sixty-four it is difficult to find a parallel in the history of music. Suddenly the sluice gate of Janáček's inspiration was opened and over the next twelve years a spate of works flooded from his pen, singularly original, each strikingly pertinent. An orchestral rhapsody inspired by Gogol's novel *Taras Bulba* (1918) was followed by a disturbing and strongly evocative song cycle *The Diary of One who Disappeared* and the tone poem *The Ballad of Blanik* (1920). But it was Janáček's special sense of drama and the value he set on dramatic music which gave him a unique insight into opera. He knew instinctively how to merge himself with the mood of each subject and how best to portray his characters. He placed the main emphasis on the singers and adopted a form of dramatic realism close to that found in Russian opera of the period. In fact Janáček was so attracted to Russian revolutionary and romantic literature that he alternated Russian and Czech themes as subjects for his compositions. Possibly *Katá Kabanová,* his sixth opera, is an expression of his love for the strength of the Russian people, for it is based on Ostrovsky's *The Storm* and is set in a narrow provincial Russian environment with the ever-moving waters of the Volga as a background to Katá's tragic longing for love.

In 1920 Janáček's fancy was captured by a newspaper supplement by Rudolf Tesnohlídek whose charming story about a sharp-eared fox prompted the composer to write *The Cunning Little Vixen,* a fantasy in which the world of people is joined with the world of animals and nature. None of the theatres in Brno or Prague seemed able to keep pace with Janáček's output; for in 1925, the year of his *Concertino* for piano and chamber orchestra, his eighth opera was ready for performance. *The Makropoulos Case,* another fantasy, this time based on Karel Capek's allegorical play, delves into the problems of prolonging life and reveals the harsh truth and profound logic of death. *The Makropoulos Case* was put into production in Brno in 1926, the year Janáček composed his *Capriccio* for piano (left hand) and wind ensemble and his *Glagolitic Mass,* a fiery, pantheistic celebration of life in all its power and glory, an outburst that can scarcely be called church music in the liturgic sense and a work in which the composer attempted to show people how to speak to God. In his seventy-third year, and with the vigour of a younger man, Janáček set to work on what was to be his final opera, *From the House of the Dead,* based on Dostoevsky's powerful novel describing the reminiscences of the aristocrat Alexander Gorianchikov, interned as a political prisoner in the Serbian penal settlement at Omst. The opera, like the novel, is a shocking document of the lot of uprooted people living in misery and wretchedness. Though it plumbs new depths of human psychology and degradation it remains a towering document of Janáček's genius as a composer of opera.

In the last years of his life Janáček began to be more widely acclaimed. He was himself an indefatigable promoter of his own works, taking an active part in the congresses of contemporary music held in Salzburg, Venice, London and Frankfurt between 1923 and 1927. Yet despite honours showered upon him at home he remained a simple man. As time went on he was drawn back to his native Moravia where he created the second *String Quartet,* subtitled 'Intimate Letters'. This was to be his last major offering, for he died suddenly following a bout of pneumonia at Ostrava in August 1928.

The man and the music

Janáček was a rare personality among composers, and an examination of one of his manuscripts quickly reveals characteristics of the man himself. A scattered shower of notes seems to spell out his passionate, excitable nature. A theme flashes across the page like forked lightning — wild, robust, rapturous. The music is subject to sharply changing moods, motivated by the stubborn, pugnacious energy of the composer's personality. For Janáček work was a creed. His knowledge and achievement were built up from nothing. He struggled with scores like *Jenufa* for more than ten years and in his seventies could pour out new works with the vitality of a man in his thirties. He was a rebel who broke with all that was old and established, yet he never lost interest in humanity. Man, intoxicated with enthusiasm, moved and inspired him. He observed his native people in the *Lachian Dances,* and portrayed their warmth and characteristics in his orchestral ballad *The Fiddler's Child;* and on reading how a Moravian lad had fallen under the spell of a hot-blooded gipsy, his understanding of love led him to create the *Diary of One Who Disappeared.* Similarly when a worker was killed by a soldier's bayonet-thrust for demonstrating for a Czech University in Brno, Janáček could not remain silent, but registered his sympathy in the *Piano Sonata October 1st,* 1905. His love of humanity was such that it led him to explore the expressive rhythms and inflexions of Moravian dialect and he attuned his ear to the elements of melodic speech curves so that he was able to deduce what nature of man was speaking. In studying 'living-speech', as he called it, Janáček jotted down snatches of motifs from tradesmen, newsboys, railway guards, waiters, even the children he heard crying in the streets. His notes, be they on a postcard, a shirt cuff or in a diary, show how he analysed the sounds of laughter, of weeping, of falling rain, of whistling wind, of bubbling brooks; and his visit to the London Zoo in 1926 opened up a new world of animal and bird noises that helped him develop a genuine musical language founded on realism. But Janáček did not impose such effects on his music mechanically: he stylised and transformed his expression in such a way that his utterance became more concise. The directness and terseness with which he moulds a motif of only a few notes is often remarkable; and its expressiveness depends as much on rhythm as it does upon melody. Janáček's music is full of life, provocative in its abrupt changes, tantalising in its unpredictability. In his technique of instrumentation Janáček appears to use the orchestra in an almost whimsical, reckless way. Often harsh woodwinds shriek against turgid bass lines while the middle cushion of orchestral sound is left unexploited. Everything is pruned down and dispensed along lines in unlikely combinations which on paper suggest that the music might sound clumsy. Far from it. In performance the music is surprisingly colourful, sometimes rough, almost primitive, but to the point, well fitted to the passionate and laconic style that was Janáček's and, from time to time, even visionary.

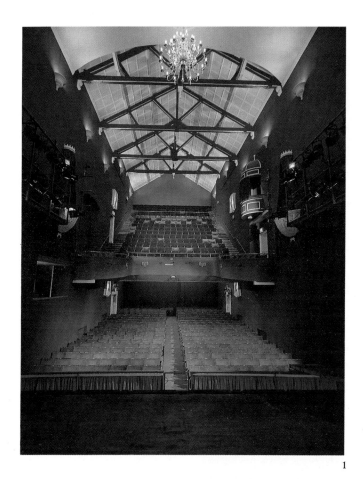

1

2

3

Pl 1 *The Theatre Royal was extensively remodelled and redecorated in 1987. It was reopened on 5 September by the then President of Ireland, Dr Patrick J Hillery, at a gala concert featuring Daniela Bechly and John O'Conor.*

Pl 2 *Wolf-Ferrari's* La Vedova Scaltra, *produced by Charles Hamilton and conducted by Yan Pascal Tortelier, with designs by Tim Reed, was staged in 1983 and featured Howard Haskin and Jill Gomez.*

Pl 3 *Daniela Bechly as the goosegirl in the 1986 production of Humperdinck's fairytale opera* Königskinder. *Albert Rosen conducted this presentation which was produced by Michael McCaffrey, with designs by Di Seymour.*

Pl 4 *Massenet's charming version of the Cinderella story,* Cendrillon, *appeared at the 1987 Festival, with Robynne Redmon as Prince Charming. Stéphane Cardon conducted, with production and sets by Seamus McGrenera and Tim Reed.*

Pl 5 *Rossini returned to Wexford in 1986 when his* Tancredi *was staged by Michael Beauchamp and William Passmore, conducted by the music director of the Drottningholm Opera, Arnold Oestman. Inga Neilsen, as Amenaide, is seen here in trouble with Urbazzano, sung by the young Finnish bass Petteri Salomaa.*

4

5

6

7

Pl 6 *Alison Browner and Miroslav Kopp in* Don Giovanni Tenorio *(1988), Gazzaniga's version of the Don Juan legend, in a Patrick Mason-Joe Vaněk production conducted by Simon Joly.*

Pl 7 *The 1983 production of Marschner's* Hans Heiling *caused quite a stir; conducted by Albert Rosen, produced by Stephen Pimlott and designed by David Fielding, it brought the Russian baritone Sergei Leiferkus to Wexford in the title role.*

Opposite:
Pl 8 *The other* Turandot, *by Busoni, was seen in 1988 and brought Kristine Ciesinski to Wexford; she is seen here with Milan Voldrich as Kalaf.*

9 10

11 12

Pl 9 *The monks of Cluny Abbey in the 1984 production of Massenet's* Le Jongleur de Notre-Dame, *a production by Stefan Janski and Johan Engels, conducted by Yan Pascal Tortelier.*

Pl 10 *Bernadette Greevy in the 1982 production of Haydn's* L'Isola Disabitata, *conducted by Newell Jenkins and staged by Guus Mostart and John Otto.*

Pl 11 *Marko Putkonen as the devil in Dvořák's opera* The Devil and Kate, *produced in 1988 by Francesca Zambello, with designs by Neil Peter Jampolis, and conducted by Albert Rosen. This presentation was video-taped and broadcast internationally.*

Pl 12 *Cynthia Clarey made a distinguished appearance as Isoletta in Bellini's early opera* La Straniera *in 1987; Jan Latham-Koenig conducted.*

13

14

Pl 13 *Karen Notare and John Cimino in the 1990 production of Leoncavallo's* Zazà.

Pl 14 *Jorge de Leon as Georges Brown in Boieldieu's* La Dame Blanche *celebrating his return to Avenel in the 1990 production produced by Jean-Claude Auvray, with sets and costumes by Kenny MacLellan.*

15

16

17 *Pl 15 Ann Murray as Laodicea and Philip Langridge as Eurimidonte in the 1975 production of Cavalli's* Eritrea. *The couple met in this production and later were married.*

Pl 16 The powerful 1989 production of Mozart's early opera Mitridate, Re di Ponto *was produced by Lucy Bailey, with designs by Peter J Davison. Here Patricia Rozario as Ismene confronts Luretta Bybee in the* travesti *role of Farnace.*

Pl 17 David Parker as the king in the lavish 1982 production of Alfano's Sakùntala, *produced by Nicholas Hytner, with designs by David Fielding.*

Pl 18 Neil Jenkins as Don Jerome tries to rehearse his group of musicians in the colourful 1989 production of Prokofiev's The Duenna, *based on Richard Brindsley Sheridan's play; Patrick Mason produced, with designs by Joe Vaněk.*

18

19

Pl 19 *Rosanne Creffield and Günter von Kannen as the devil and his wife, trying to tempt the innocent Grisélidis (Rosemarie Landry) in the 1982 production of Massenet's opera.*

20

Pl 20 *Alexander Oliver as Prunier in Puccini's* La Rondine *(1971); he also made a considerable impression as Albert Herring in Britten's opera, staged the previous year.*

Pl 21 *The symbolic presentation of Marschner's* Der Templer und die Jüdin *(1989) by Francesca Zambello, with designer Bettina Munzer, proved highly controversial; here Anita Soldh, as Rebecca, is tried for witchcraft by the Knights Templar. The opera is an adaptation of Scott's* Ivanhoe.

21

1950-1960

Above: *Left to right: Veronica Dunne, famous Irish soprano, Nicola Monti and Elvina Ramella, at a reception in White's Hotel after the performance of* Don Pasquale *in 1953.*

Left: *From the 1951 production of* The Rose of Castile: *James Browne, Murray Dickie and Michael Hanlon.*

Far Right: *Bass Giorgio Tadeo as Gottardo in Rossini's* La Gazza Ladra *(1959)*

Right: *Paolo Pedani made an impressive Doge in the 1958 production of Verdi's* I Due Foscari.

Maria Casula as Sextus and Peter Baillie as Titus in the second Mozart opera to be staged at the Festival, La Clemenza di Tito *(1968).*

1960-1970

Top left: *The remarkable French tenor, Alain Vanzo, came to Wexford for the 1961 production of Gounod's* Mireille; *he is seen here with Andrea Guiot and Jean Borthayre.*

Top right: *The 1966 production of Auber's* Fra Diavolo *starred Ugo Benelli with Antonio Boyer and Anna Reynolds.*

Bottom left: *The Norwegian tenor Ragnar Ulfung, who took the title role in Verdi's* Ernani *(1961)*

Bottom right: *Lino Puglisi played Don Carlos in the 1961 production of Verdi's* Ernani, *conducted by Bryan Balkwill, produced by Peter Ebert and designed by Reginald Woolley.*

Don Pasquale was revived in 1963 with a cast which included Alfonz Bartha (Ernesto) and Birgit Nordin (Norina).

Theodor Guschlbauer conducted the 1968 presentation of Mozart's La Clemenza di Tito *in a cast which included Hanneke van Bork, Maria Casula and Delia Wallis.*

Daniel Auber (1782-1871), the long-lived French composer whose comedy Fra Diavolo *was seen at the 1966 Festival.*

Aldo Ceccato conducted the 1968 production of Rossini's L'Equivoco Stravagante *which was produced by John Cox and designed by John Stoddart.*

In 1968 Denise Dupleix appeared as Cathrine Glover, the eponymous Jolie Fille de Perth *in a production of Bizet's opera conducted by David Lloyd-Jones.*

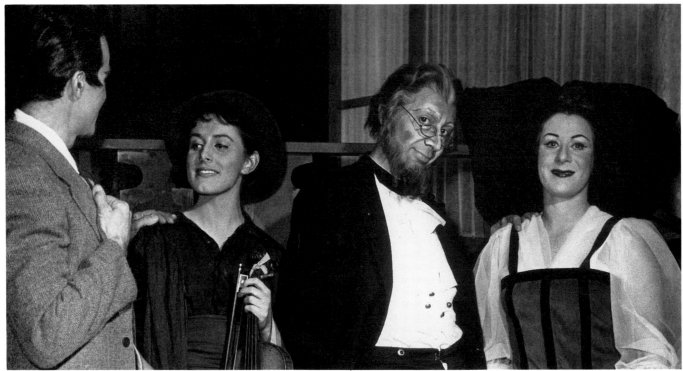

L'Amico Fritz *in 1962 brought together two great Irish singers, seen here with their Italian colleagues: Nicola Monti, Bernadette Greevy, Paolo Pedani and Veronica Dunne.*

Donizetti's Lucia di Lammermoor *was seen at the 1964 Festival, with Franco Ventriglia as Raimondo and Giacomo Aragall as Edgardo. Antonio de Almeida conducted.*

One of the few popular operas to be staged at the Festival was Donizetti's Lucia di Lammermoor *(1964) in Reginald Woolley's magic sets, conducted by Antinio de Almeida. Karola Agai took the part of the unfortunate Bride of Lammermoor.*

The other version of Otello, by Rossini, was staged in 1967 with Nicola Tagger as the Moor of Venice and Renza Jotti as Desdamona. Albert Rosen conducted, with sets by John Stoddart, in a production by Anthony Besch.

Peter Baillie as Titus in Mozart's La Clemenza di Tito, *produced by John Copley, settings by Michael Waller.*

Bernadette Greevy and a pair of well-behaved wolfhounds in the 1969 presentation of Verdi's Luisa Miller, *conducted by Myer Fredman, produced by John Cox, with settings by Bernard Culshaw.*

The Mayor of Loxford (Patrick Ring) at the May Day celebrations in Britten's Albert Herring *1970.*

Alexander Oliver as Albert after his downfall in Michael Geliot's 1970 production of Albert Herring, *conducted by David Atherton.*

Top, from left:

The popular Scottish conductor Roderick Brydon appeared at the 1974 Festival to conduct Mayr's Medea in Corinto.

The German-born producer Axel Bartz, who was brought up in Australia, designed the 1978 production of Haydn's Il Mondo della Luna.

Kenneth Montgomery, now artistic director of Opera Northern Ireland in his native Belfast, first conducted in Wexford in 1971 (Il Re Pastore) and returned for the 1972 (Oberon) and 1973 (L'Ajo nell'Imbarazzo) seasons.

Belgian conductor Guy Barbier paid two visits to Wexford, firstly for the 1971 production of Bozet's Les Pêcheurs de Perles and again in 1973 for the memorable presentation of Glinka's Ivan Susanin, with Matti Salminen and the young Dennis O'Neill as a messenger.

British soprano Felicity Palmer made her operatic debut in Houston in 1970 and came to Wexford in 1978 to play Aneska in the production of Smetana's The Two Widows.

American tenor Robert White appeared as Lasilav in the 1978 production of Smetana's The Two Widows, conducted by Albert Rosen and produced by David Pountney. It was a co-production with Scottish Opera, who later toured their production in Scotland.

Centre, from left:

James Maguire was the first home-produced 'star' when he astonished 1976 audiences with his rounded interpretation of Miles in Britten's The Turn of the Screw at the age of fourteen.

Designer Roger Butlin first came to the Festival in 1974 for Massenet's Thaïs and returned as designer for Tiefland (1978) and La Vestale (1979).

Jill Gomez was one of the most popular visitors to the Festival in the early 1970s. She made her debut in 1969 (L'Infedelta Delusa) and returned for the l970 double bill and as the heroine of the fine 1974 production of Massenet's Thaïs.

1970-1980

Top left: *Ugo Benelli and Jill Gomez in the 1970 production of Rossini's one-act comedy* L'Inganno Felice.

Top right: *Bizet's charming* Les Pêcheurs de Perles *(1971) saw the return of Christiane Eda-Pierre to the Festival. Guy Barbier conducted with sets by Roger Butlin and costumes by Jane Bond.*

Left: Les Pêcheurs de Perles *(1971)*

Bottom right: The American soprano Vivian Martin played Rezia, the heroine of Weber's Oberon, *in 1972, conducted by Kenneth Montgomery.*

Elizabeth Dalton's sets for John Cox's production of Il Re Pastore *were greatly admired. Norma Burrowes and Anne Pashley were featured in this, the second Mozart opera to be staged at the Festival.*

The Finnish tenor Heikki Siukola as Huon, the hero of Oberon *(1972).*

Joseph Rouleau as the General, reads a letter in Prokofiev's The Gambler *(1973), watched by Richard Stilgoe, Bernard Dickerson and Anne Howells.*

Jill Gomez, the distinguished soprano from British Guiana, made her third appearance at the Festival in the title role of Thaïs *in 1974, conducted by Jacques Delacôte.*

Left: *Richard McKee as the tutor with the Argentinian soprano Silvia Baleani in Patrick Libby's 1973 production of Donizetti's comedy,* L'Ajo nell'Imbarazzo.

Above: *Gillian Knight and Stuart Harling in Bernard Arnould's atmospheric setting for the 1975 production of Lalo's* Le Roi d'Ys.

Right: *Eurimidonte (Philip Langridge) faces Laodicea (Ann Murray) in the 1975 presentation of the earliest opera ever staged at the Festival, Cavalli's* Eritrea. *The two singers first met on this occasion and later were married. Also in the scene is Anne Pashley, Paul Esswood and John York Skinner.*

Above: *The 1977 production of Massenet's* Hérodiade *starred Bernadette Greevy, Bonaventura Bottone and Alvaro Malta.*

Bottom left: *Dacre Punt designed the settings for the controversial 1977 production by Wolf Siegfried Wagner of Gluck's* Orfeo ed Euridice. *Jennifer Smith was the heroine and Kevin Smith the hero; Jane Glover returned to conduct the opera following her debut with* Eritrea *in 1975.*

Bottom right: *One of the most sought-after producers today is David Pountney. He made his debut at Wexford in 1972 with a remarkable presentation of Janáček's* Kata Kabanová, *conducted by Albert Rosen, with sets by Maria Blane and Maria Bjornsen. His later productions have included* The Gambler *and* The Two Widows.

Above: *Gasparo Spontini's* La Vestale *was written in 1803 and was staged at the 1979 Festival in a setting by Roger Butlin. The Israeli soprano Mani Mekler as Julia places the wreath on the head of Licinius (Ennio Buoso), watched by Roderick Kennedy and Terence Sharpe.*

Left: *Montemezzi's* L'amore dei Tre Re *provides a great role for a basso. Alvaro Malta appeared as the blind King Archibaldo in the 1979 production which was conducted by Pinchas Steinberg.*

1980-1990

American tenor Curtis Rayam endeared himself to the Wexford Festival both on and off the stage. He made his debut in the 1976 opera Giovanna d'Arco *(Verdi) as the King of France, with the Japanese soprano Emiko Maruyama as Giovanna, and the Hungarian baritone Lajos Miller as her father. He has returned to Wexford on a number of occasions, most memorably as Lennie in Carlisle Floyd's opera* Of Mice and Men *(1980).*

Patrick Power was born into an Irish family in New Zealand and holds dual nationality. He made his Wexford debut in 1984 in the title role of Massenet's Le Jongleur de Notre-Dame.

American composer Carlisle Floyd visited the 1980 Festival for the highly successful performance of his opera Of Mice and Men, *which starred tenor Curtis Rayam.*

The imposing figure of the young Finnish bass Petteri Salomaa was a feature of the 1985 production of Handel's Ariodante; *he returned the following year for* Tancredi *(Rossini).*

French conductor Yan Pascal Tortelier first came to Ireland as a violinist in the company of his father, Paul Tortelier, the great cellist. He made his conducting debut with Wolf-Ferrari's La Vedova Scaltra *(1983) and returned for* Le Jongleur de Notre-Dame *(1984) and* Mignon *(1986). He extended his Irish activities when he became principal conductor of the Ulster Orchestra and he is a frequent visitor to Belfast.*

Left: *The great Kirov baritone Sergei Leiferkus made his Western European debut as the Marquis in Massenet's* Grisélidis *(1982) and has returned to the Festival for further operas and recitals, including* Hans Heiling *(Marschner) in 1983 and* Königskinder *(1986).*

Above: *The noted American musicologist and conductor Newell Jenkins came to Wexford to direct the Haydn double bill in 1982.*

In 1982 the Festival continued its distinguished series of Massenet revivals with Grisélidis. *The production was later taken on tour around Ireland, with Neil Jansen as the Marquis and Joan Merrigan in the title role.*

The young Argentinian tenor, Raul Gimenez, made his Wexford debut as Filandro in Cimarosa's Le Astuzie Femminili *at the 1984 Festival.*

Opposite: *Cilea's* La Wally *sprang to renewed fame with the 1981 French cult thriller* Diva. *Wexford staged it in 1985 with Josella Ligi in the title role, and sets by Marie-Jeanne Lecca.*

Opposite: Kathleen Kuhlmann and Inga Neilsen as Tancredi and Amenaide in the 1986 production of Rossini's opera conducted by Arnold Oestman.

Top : Pauline Tinsley as the witch and Daniela Bechly as the goose-girl in the 1986 production of Humperdinck's Königskinder.

Bottom: Joan Davies had been a frequent performer at the Festival, in particular bringing her fine comic talent to a number of productions, most recently in the 1988 double bill.

The colourful production of Prokofiev's
The Duenna, *a setting of Richard*
Brindsley Sheridan's play, was
designed by Joe Vaněk and produced
by Patrick Mason in 1989.

FAMOUS VISITORS

Joan Davies, Ian Caddy and Eric Garrett in the 1975 production of Rossini's La Pietra del Paragone

Wexford's other delights

by Andrew Porter

As music critic of The New Yorker, **Andrew Porter** *is one of the world's leading critics and has had the rare distinction of having his reviews compiled and published in book form. For many years he was a regular visitor to Wexford and was one of the international writers who helped place the Festival on the world opera map. He chose the following piece from among his many contributions.*

*A*s the music critic of The Financial Times *I visited the Wexford Festival regularly almost from its inception and told readers each year of the delight of discovering unfamiliar works, hearing new young singers, and responding to opera that was so vitally, directly and intimately presented. Twenty years ago, the BBC invited me to tell also of the extra-musical pleasures that conspired to make each Wexford visit memorable; and this little tribute is based on that talk. I was back in Wexford last year, after far too long away, and found that some things had changed much, others hardly at all. The work of Harry Clarke, I learnt, is more widely appreciated today than it was twenty years ago; Selskar Abbey is no longer neglected, overgrown and accessible only with persistence; above all, my earlier description of the Theatre Royal was no longer accurate. With local help, I have removed what is no longer applicable. Unchanged was a sense of keen delight in the place and an eagerness to embark on new voyages of discovery.*

One of the rewards of a music critic's life is the chance it brings of exploring new landscapes, discovering new towns, entering new buildings. Professionally I may be off to, say, Harrogate, for a few days of festival; privately I leap at the chance of visiting Fountains and Byland, Riveaulx and Jervaulx, and following steps traced by Dr August Bozzi Glanville in his fascinating book about English spas. I'm delighted when Glasgow announces some première or important new production: that city takes a lot of getting to know, and preparation will involve collecting information such as where exactly the ex-convent of Downhill is and whether its Harry Clarke windows are still there.

And so with Wexford, which the *Shell Guide* rightly calls 'a place of considerable attraction to the tourist and to the antiquarian'. Although I have been going to Wexford for many years, there are still dozens of places around it that I want to visit, dozens of things to do there that I have still not got round to doing. It's not in every town that you can go into the local Woolworths and ask to be shown the 'murder hole' that was installed when Cromwell made his headquarters there. At Festival time a series of tours is laid on for visitors. For many years they were conducted by that passionate local historian Dr George Haddon, and the tradition continues. The snag has been matching the days of a Festival visit to the tour schedule. I've so far missed excursions with such irresistibly romantic titles as 'Into the mists of prehistory: Ratha Speck, Lady's Island, and Bally Trent' or 'Ten feet below the sea: Mulgannon and South Slob'.

But first there is the equally pleasant business of getting there. Wexford is about eighty miles south of Dublin, a hundred miles east of Cork. The visitor from abroad can go by boat from Fishguard or begin by flying to Dublin, proceeding on by bus or train, or hiring a car. Then a tantalising choice of routes lies open, most of them marked on the map with the green shading that indicates 'beautiful landscape'. My favourite route runs through the Vale of Avoca. Long before I first visited Ireland, John McCormack had told me that 'There's not in this wide world a valley so sweet as that vale in whose bosom the bright waters meet.' And there it lies before one for real. There's just one dead tree in the landscape, not cut down because, we are told, beneath it Tom Moore (whose mother, incidentally, was Wexford-born) wrote those famous lines. On the way

Soprano Sandra Browne has the final touches put to her wig in the 1975 production of La Pietra del Paragone *(Rossini).*

Ian Caddy prepares for his appearance as Pacuvio in the 1975 production of Rossini's La Pietra del Paragone.

there is also Glendalough: a picturesque series of ruins in a glen where two lakes meet, what remains of a monastic city, founded by St Kevin in the sixth century, that was renowned throughout Europe. This is a fine collection, in a wild, romantic setting, of early Irish architecture.

Further south, if you have chosen one of the eastern routes, you reach Gorey in County Wexford, and this is the place to start getting the eye in for Victorian Ireland, dominated by Augustus Welby Pugin. There are two Pugin churches in Gorey, both dating from about 1840, but in different styles. One thinks of Pugin as essentially a Gothic revivalist, but St Mark's is an essay in the Norman manner. In the Anglican cathedral is a Harry Clarke window of St Stephen. On to the town of Ferns, and back to the thirteenth century for the ruined cathedral and one of the best castles in the Norman-Irish style. A few miles on is Enniscorthy and another castle, Norman-built, repaired in 1586; Edmund Spenser once lived here. Now it houses one of those delightful jumbly museums where objects of all kinds — from fragments of an old stone cross to a ten-inch nail — have been gratefully accepted and carefully labelled. Enniscorthy also has a handsome Gothic cathedral, St Aidan's, by Pugin. It's tempting to dally. Suddenly you realise that if you don't get a move on you may not reach the opera in time.

From Gorey, a direct road can take you straight to Wexford, across the mouth of the River Slaney by a modern bridge. The leisurely approach through Ferns and Enniscorthy is more romantic. It crosses the Slaney about three miles inland, where the wide, flat river suddenly narrows to flow strongly between steep, wooded heights. This is a beautiful place, especially in the evening, perhaps best of all in the early dawn light if, after the Festival, you have taken the early train back to Dublin and morning mists are lifting off the river as it is caught by the sun.

At first glimpse, Wexford may suggest a fishing port rather than a county town. A wide river, calm as a lake; gulls wheeling and screaming; modest houses along the quay; white-washed walls; slate roofs — all huddled beneath an enormous sky pierced by two Gothic spires. Wexford streets are narrow, Wexford houses are small, and essentially the town has the structure of the trading settlement beside a natural harbour which was established in the ninth century by the Norse invaders — those Vikings who wasted Ireland's

monasteries and created Dublin, Waterford and Wexford. When Ptolemy drew his map of the world, in Alexandria in AD 150, he called the place Menapia. Wexford itself is a Danish name, *Waes-fjord*, which means *Harbour of the Mud Flats*.

The Normans arrived in the twelfth century, and Wexford was the first fortified town to fall before their assault. The invaders were repelled at first, but the following day, so we are told, their leader Robert Fitzstephen, said: 'To go home with nothing done would be ruin, a blot on the valour of England as well as a disgrace to ourselves', and so when the English landed and attacked again, he burnt their boats behind them. Wexford's coat-of-arms today is still three blazing ships. Not many ships around now; the port has silted up. Today it is used mainly for sailing, crab fishing, and even water-skiing. One of the largest remaining boats, a converted lightship, is a nautical museum commemorating the days when Wexford was a flourishing port.

The architecture is still largely Georgian: not one of those carefully planned Georgian towns like Westport in County Mayo, not a neat garrison town like Birr, but a little town that has grown up slowly, with some rebuilding here, some patching there, along the old street plan and within the city walls, bounded by the river and by the long straight hill behind. High Street and Main Street run its length, twisting a little as they follow the natural lie of the land. They are scarcely wide enough for two cars. At Festival time, strings of coloured lights are hung along them, from one house window to another. The streets converge on the Bullring, the site of Cromwell's massacre, where there's a statue of a young Wexford pikeman. Lanes, alleys and short streets link them, running down to the waterfront. Wandering through the town, you find ruins of three old churches that Cromwell destroyed. The most notable and picturesque is that of Selskar Abbey. Henry II did penance here, in 1169, for the murder of Thomas Becket. Cromwell sacked it in 1649. Early in the nineteenth century the chancel and tower were rebuilt as an Anglican church, but this in turn was unroofed in 1961.

The most notable eighteenth-century building is the Anglican church of St Iberius, a handsome, spacious building where Festival artists often sing Sunday service. Close to the Theatre Royal is one of the two Gothic churches whose spires dominate the town: the Church of the

Immaculate Conception and the Church of the Assumption. They are called the twin churches because they are almost identical. The architect was not Pugin (he designed the chapel of St Peter's College) but his pupil and assistant Robert Pierce. And in the Church of the Assumption is the single work of art most worth seeing in Wexford: a memorial window by that most brilliant and inventive of modern artists in stained glass, Harry Clarke.

Outside Ireland, Harry Clarke is probably most famous as a book illustrator, one who could be loosely described as a successor to Beardsley. (Goethe's *Faust* and Edgar Allan Poe's *Tales* are among his most prized books). But his genius was for stained glass: for a control of colour, of light, of strange thrilling design that is unlike anything else I know. He was born in Dublin in 1889, and he died in Davos, Switzerland, in 1931. There is not much of his work in Britain: the Glasgow windows mentioned earlier, a marvellous series of lancets and a great three-light window in Notre Dame Convent in Ashdown Park, Surrey. But in Ireland there is a good deal of his work to be seen. After winning several prizes, he visited Chartres on a scholarship; on return he destroyed his previous work and resolved to create nothing that did not have the depth and resonance of medieval glass. His first big commission, in 1915, was for eight windows in the Honan Hostel Chapel, Cork. One year I approached Wexford in a roundabout way, through Cork, in order to see them.

The Wexford window is also early, dated 1919, and in memory of Lieutenant William Henry O'Keefe RFA, who was killed in action over France in 1917. It's a two-light window. On the left, the Virgin and Child; on the right, St Patrick and St George. The large figures float in heaven, gleaming, jewelled, and mysterious, and below them is France at war: a landscape with an aeroplane flying over it; the coast; little ships. Ruskin once wrote that 'the true perfection of a painted window is to be serene, intense, brilliant like flaming jewellery, full of easily legible and quaint subjects, and exquisitely subtle yet simple in its harmonies'. He was thinking of Chartres, but he could have been describing the Wexford window.

Of course, the extra-musical pleasures of Wexford are found not only in buildings and history and stained-glass. The brochures tell of midnight fishing, hurling matches, motor races, a singing competition in the pubs. (There are supposed to be over a hundred pubs in the two main streets; I wonder who counted). For bird lovers, there is the North Slob, where 80 per cent of the world's population of white-fronted geese spend the winter. The trees in the John F Kennedy Arboretum, twenty miles to the west, are growing taller. Always more to do, whatever your interests, than there is time for! Much is omitted from this little sketch. I resolve that next time I will be sure to allow a few hours on the trip back to see the Harry Clarke window in Arklow, and approach Dublin through Rathfarnham, where there are eight late windows in the chapel of the former Jesuit retreat house.

Wexford Gaiety

by Desmond Shawe-Taylor

Desmond Shawe-Taylor *is widely regarded as the doyen of music critics, and Wexford was fortunate that he was an early and enthusiastic visitor to the Festival. He has continued to promote it right up to the present day and has selected this early article, which appeared in* New Statesman *on 9 November 1957, as an example of the kind of report he made of early productions, which had already reached a high degree of excellence in the first decade of the Festival.*

Of all the Festivals that stipple the map of Europe, that of Wexford is surely the most festive. The organisers realise that a Festival is something more than a string of concerts and opera performances; it ought by rights to be − and here it is − a kind of carnival. Wexford offers all the simple gregarious pleasures short of dancing in the streets; and no doubt we should have had that too but for those autumn puddles reflecting the washed blue sky.

The pretty harbour town, its narrow streets illuminated in the Italian fashion with festoons of coloured lights, is caught up for a whole week in a whirl of enthusiasm and hospitality, opera talk and conviviality of all sorts. It never goes to bed. I wish the Edinburgh Fathers would nip across and take a look at the very thing which their own grand and dignified Festival so notably lacks: the party spirit. So far from being thrown out in the cold at ten sharp, or denied a drink altogether on a Sunday, we are welcome to celebrate wherever we like at all hours. Around three o'clock, in the lounge of the Talbot, a District Justice launches into a long and entertaining ditty about the price of a heifer. Soon the Italian singers will be along, fortified by huge plates of spaghetti, to join in the Irish folk-songs with shouts of glee, and to oblige with a few assorted arias of their own. Spontaneous fun bubbles; the great national sport of 'codding' is indulged on all sides; Wexford, in short, is the best place to forget all about satellites and the arms race and the wage freeze.

Don't run away with the idea that music comes second in the scheme of things. Not at all. The success of the Wexford Festival is firmly based on the traditional partiality of the Irish for Italian opera. In the nineteenth century there used to be long Italian seasons in Dublin, with very fine singers in the casts; to realise how the affinity has persisted we have only to think of James Joyce, Bernard Shaw, John McCormack. Voices are what the Irish love and have always loved: their own to begin with, then the rolling theatrical periods of Synge and O'Casey, most of all the sweet lilt of melodious song. It is the achievement of an amateur, a Wexford doctor named Tom Walsh, to have canalised this national passion. Dr Walsh has an intense enthusiasm for opera and a good ear for a voice; in the selection of singers he has been sometimes helped by the local postman, a shy man who would not care to read his name in print, but who sets off every now and then for La Scala and chooses well. Leaning a little on Glyndebourne for musical and production staff and chorus stiffening, the Wexford team has put on a week of opera for the last seven years: mainly Italian, but sometimes German; originally one opera each year, and now two. This year the choice fell on Donizetti's *La Figlia del Reggimento* and Rossini's *L'Italiana in Algeri.* Next year there may be a rare Verdi and a still rarer Rossini.

There is much point, over and above the national predilection, in sticking to this school and period of opera. Performances are given in the little Theatre Royal, which, when crammed to bursting (its normal Festival state), seats only about 440. In the early nineteenth century it must have been a pretty house with stage boxes, and many famous actors have played there; at some time it was converted into a cinema, with damage which might have been worse if the converters had had more money. Even now, as soon as we are inside, we recognise that this is the kind of theatre from which Rossini and Donizetti sprang,

123

for which they mostly wrote. As in old theatrical prints, the audience is on top of the orchestra (Radio Éireann Light Orchestra, doing not too badly in a field outside their usual round), and could shake hands with the characters — often look, indeed, as though they would like to. A spirit of rare intimacy and shared enjoyment reigns: something quite different from Glyndebourne because it is popular and devil-may-care. We comprehend, as the overture strikes up nearly half an hour late, how Rossini, like Aristophanes, grew up in a world of local jokes and private scandals; how, as Stendhal relates, an actor might well happen to have been imitating on the stage the local bore who that moment was entering his box, sublimely unaware of the situation. Not that this happened at Wexford, where there seem to be no local bores, and, alas, no boxes.

Graziella Sciutti was the heroine of *The Daughter of the Regiment,* and made it clear why this opera was once so popular with audiences and with singers like Jenny Lind and Marcella Sembrich. Just as *L'Elisir d'Amore* gives the sentimental Italian tenor a much-cherished chance to play the fool, so *Figlia* allows the brilliant high soprano to romp around the stage in uniform, swear prettily — and then melt in two or three arias of tender sweetness, of which the best known is 'Convien partir'. Mme Sciutti sang with great verve and charm, and made a captivating *vivandière* to the eye — though it was a pity she didn't play a little sidedrum in the traditional style. She was well supported by the clear-toned and upstanding Tonio of Mario Spina, and by a typically clever sketch of the bluff Sergeant Sulpizio from Geraint Evans.

One thing partially marred our pleasure in both operas: the excessive volume (unnecessary in so small a house)

produced almost continually by chorus, orchestra and most of the soloists. I was told that this effect was due to the position of my seat at *Figlia,* and was sedulously placed elsewhere for *L'Italiana,* which is not an opera that lends itself so easily to bawling. But even here, in the very first scene, Paolo Montarsolo (who had also sung Mustafà at Glyndebourne) all but broke my ear-drums — ironically enough, in the phrase 'Cara, m'hai rotto il timpano' addressed to his complaining wife. The crazy finale to Act 1, which went splendidly, is the one place in which a deafening volume has real dramatic point. But in general I think that the very able conductor, Bryan Balkwill, ought to ponder this question of appropriate volume-levels seriously, because the lack of a real hush banished some of the magic from several lyrical episodes, especially in the Donizetti score. In the Rossini, Petre Munteanu was allowed to sing his tenor music very sweetly, and made a great effect. Barbara Howitt, hampered by a sore throat, coped creditably with the difficulties of the title-role. I am sorry to add that Peter Ebert's production, already disfigured by some crudities at Glyndebourne, had become shamelessly self-indulgent at Wexford: characters were made to jig in time to the music (this is the worst Ebert trade-mark) in almost every number of the second act. Joseph Carl's sets were simple and pleasing. The modest scheme of the Festival was filled out by several opera and ballet films and some admirably chosen straight films, including that Italian masterpiece, *Amici per la pelle*; also by a number of recitals, of which those by Gina Bachauer and Anna Raquel Satre aroused particular interest.

(Reprinted, with permission, from *The New Statesman and Nation*.)

WEXFORD FUN

Rossini's delightful comedy L'Equivoco Stravagante *(1968) was presented in a hilarious production by John Cox. It featured Maria Casula, Richard van Allan and Elfego Esparza.*

Recipe for a Rossini overture

by Spike Hughes

Patrick Cairns 'Spike' Hughes *(1908-1987) was one of the leading writers on music and opera over the last forty years. Originally a successful jazz musician, he went on to write books on Mozart, Puccini, Verdi, Toscanini and the history of Glyndebourne, as well as a popular humorous sporting series starting with* The Art of Coarse Cricket. *His delightful example of Rossini's wit appeared in the 1968 Festival programme.*

The trouble about Rossini is that having been such an unusually humorous and witty man, he has over the years become the subject of countless anecdotes involving episodes he never took part in, and been credited with a great many epigrams and cynical witticisms he never made. Most of these anecdotes and epigrams, whether authentic or spurious, have one thing in common, however: a strong element of the self-mockery – half serious, half flippant – which was so characteristic of Rossini throughout his life.

Some years ago, I found in a Naples journal of 1848, an account of a correspondence between Rossini and an unnamed gentleman which I do not think is at all widely known. Rossini's witty, typically light-hearted, self-mocking reply, was to a man who, having heard him 'frequently well spoken of', secretly wrote to the *illustre maestro* in the following terms:

My dear sir,

You have the general reputation of being a maestro who is great, obliging and an epicure. To the epicure I send herewith a terrine of pâté de foie gras de Strasbourg; to the great and obliging maestro I address the hope that he will be gracious enough to grant my request to help one of his future rivals. I have a nephew who is a musician and does not know how to write the overture to the opera he has written. Would you, who have composed so much, please be so kind as to let me know your recipe? If you were still concerned with the joys of applause my request might perhaps be indiscreet, but now that you have renounced all claims to glory, you should no longer be jealous of anybody.

I am, dear Signor Rossini, yours, etc.

Rossini, who was living at that time in retirement in Bologna, was plainly very touched by the present of a terrine of the most essential ingredient of *tournedos Rossini* and replied by return of post in terms of almost equally florid formality:

I consider myself greatly flattered, *o signore*, by the preference you show for my recipes over those of my colleagues in your concern for the embarrassing position in which your nephew finds himself. But first of all I must tell you that I have never written anything if there was any possible means of avoiding it. I do not understand what pleasure can be derived from giving oneself a headache, getting cramp in one's hand and developing a fever merely to amuse a public whose greatest delight is to be bored stiff by every effort to entertain it.

I am not, and never have been, in any way a champion of the right to work, and I find that the most beautiful and precious of all human rights is that of doing nothing. I am able to indulge in this since acquiring, not thanks to my operas but to one or two happy financial speculations (without my knowledge) I was made a party, the incomparable privilege, the right *par excellence*, the right above all rights: that of doing nothing. If, then, I have any really practical advice to offer your nephew, it is to emulate me in this rather than in anything else.

If, however, he still persists in his bizarre and inconceivable notion of wanting to work, then I will tell you the principal recipes which I had to use during the miserable period when I, too, was forced to do something. Your nephew will be able to choose the one that suits him best.

FIRST GENERAL AND INVARIABLE RULE

Wait for the eve of the first performance before composing the overture. Nothing is better for inspiration than necessity, the presence of a copyist waiting for your work, sheet by sheet, and the sinister spectacle of the impresario tearing his hair in desperation. All true masterpieces have always been written in this way. In Italy, in my time, all impresarios were as bald as the palm of your hand at thirty.

SECOND RECIPE

I wrote the overture to *Otello* in a small room in Barbaja's palace in Naples, where the fiercest and baldest of all impresarios locked me in by force, with a plate of boiled macaroni swimming in water and with no seasoning, threatening that I should not leave the room alive until I had finished the last note of the overture. You can try this recipe on your nephew, but, whatever happens, don't let him smell the delicious smell of the pâté de foie gras de Strasbourg — this kind of delicacy is suitable only for composers who do nothing, and I thank you very much for honouring me with the present you have sent me.

THIRD RECIPE

I wrote the overture to *La gazza ladra* not on the eve, but on the very day, of the first performance, up under the roof of La Scala in Milan, where I was sent by an impresario just as bad and almost as bald as Barbaja, and watched over by four stagehands. This quartet of executioners had been ordered to throw my overture, phrase by phrase, out of the window to the copyists in the courtyard below, who then delivered the parts to the first violin to rehearse. In the event of there being no pages of music to throw into the courtyard, the barbarians had orders to throw *me* to the copyists. The loft of your house, dear sir, could be used for the same purpose in the case of your nephew. God forbid that he should ever suffer any bigger falls. [Rossini was making a pun here with the word *'cadute'*, which in Italian means 'falls' but also — in the theatrical sense — 'flops'].

FOURTH RECIPE

I did better with the overture to *The Barber of Seville*. I did not write it specially to take the place of the one originally written for this extremely *buffa* opera; instead, I used another, composed for *Elisabetta, Regina d'Inghilterra,* an opera excessively *seria.* The public was enchanted by this solution. Your nephew, who has so far written no overture for this new opera, might well try this and use an overture he has already composed.

FIFTH RECIPE

I composed the overture, or rather the instrumental introduction, to *Le Comte Ory* fishing with a rod, with my feet in the water at Petit-Bourg in the company of M Aguado, who never ceased, the entire time I was fishing, to talk to me about Spanish finance, which I found indescribably tedious. I do not imagine for a moment, sir, that in similar circumstances your conversation would have anything like the same unnerving effect on the imagination of your nephew.

SIXTH RECIPE

I found myself in the same sort of nerve-shattering situation when I wrote the overture to *William Tell* in an apartment I occupied in the Boulevard Mont-Martre. Here, night and day, the queerest characters in the whole of Paris would wander in and out, smoking, drinking, chattering, shouting, bawling in my ears while I went on composing and trying to hear as little as possible. I am certain that in spite of cultural progress in France you will nevertheless still succeed in finding as many imbeciles in Paris capable of stimulating your nephew in the same way.

SEVENTH RECIPE

In the case of *Mosè* I composed no overture at all, and this is the easiest thing of all. I am quite sure that your nephew could use this final recipe with success. It is roughly the same as that adopted by my good friend Meyerbeer in *Robert le Diable* and *Les Huguenots,* and it appears that he has found it most satisfactory. I am assured that he as made use of it in *Le Prophète* as well and is full of praise for the efficacy of this recipe.

With my best wishes for the glory of your nephew and my thanks for the pâté, which I found excellent, believe me to be, etc.

Rossini,
ex-composer

A day at the races

by John Higgins

John Higgins, *the distinguished arts editor of* The Times *and author of a number of books on music, including one on the preparation of a Glyndebourne production, is yet another ambassador for the Festival. One of the open secrets of the Festival is the excellent entertainment and ambience that surround each season, and he has chosen to highlight his particular favourite in this specially written reminiscence.*

Cartographers and people of a literal turn of mind will be quick to tell you that the Rosslare road out of Wexford is not the one to take if you are intending to go to the races. They will point out with a sigh that Rosslare is the closest spot in the county to the British mainland, and therefore lies to the east, whereas the horses gallop on the way to New Ross in the west.

All this ignores the fact that a good lunch should always precede the races, and the best lunch to be found hereabouts is at the Strand Hotel, Rosslare. Its habitués always refer to it as 'Kelly's', in honour of the dynasty which built the original stern red-brick building and has been running it excellently ever since.

So it was the Rosslare road we took, I and my companion who, for reasons to be explained later, shall be called Archie. Wexford races on a Thursday, and the event should coincide with the second day of the Opera Festival. Occasionally, because of some quirk of the racing calendar or control by the phases of the moon, it is all over before the Festival opens, and in such years I have always suspected that musical standards drop a little. But in 1977 there was no problem. Archie was a festival director by profession, which is not a bad job if you can get it. During the Festival itself and the period running up to it the nights may not provide too many hours of untroubled sleep, but for the remaining months of the year you can, with a little luck, travel the world, attending other people's festivals on the pretext of perhaps picking up something to bring back for your own. Archie's festival took place on the other side of the world, so it was unlikely that he would be signing up singers and sets, lock, stock and barrel. But he had been told that Wexford was a good spot to be at the end of October. And here he was.

Thursday's lunch was excellent, and the bottle of claret from Billy Kelly's carefully controlled cellar even better. Queen's Pudding was available for dessert – where nowadays outside the most traditional of gentlemen's clubs in Pall Mall would you find Queen's Pudding? That demanded a half bottle of Sauternes.

Even so, we arrived at the racecourse with enough time to glance through the runners and riders for the three o'clock race. We had parked the car in the field opposite the track, taking care to have it facing downhill, as it had been raining for much of the previous week and it would be humiliating, as well as delaying, to have to call up a tractor to haul our wheels out of the mud at the end of the day. In the betting ring Archie's attention was caught by the board of Padraig O'Mahoney, which had a notice reading:

BET IN STERLING
PAID OUT IN STERLING

In those days there was a substantial difference in the exchange rate and the offer was well worth taking up. Selecting the winner of our race presented rather more difficulty. A number of the runners had utterly unpronounceable names, sometimes of three or more words, of Gaelic origin. They were ruled out, as Archie did not want to risk making a verbal fool of himself or have to stub his finger against the board to indicate the chosen horse. There was one animal who caused no difficulty: it was called River Slaney.

Now Archie was already well acquainted with the River Slaney. It flowed past his hotel, and when he had checked in the previous afternoon he had seen it from his room. Or rather part of it. The view was obstructed by two cleaning ladies who were busy vacuuming not the carpet but the large plate-glass window overlooking the estuary. After watching this for a couple of minutes Archie dared ask them what they were doing, and received the reply: 'Sure and we're suckin' up the flies.' When they had gone he found that this was a necessary operation. After feasting on whatever the combination of sea and Slaney had thrown up on the shore beneath the hotel, the flies retired for a siesta, or perhaps a little breeding, to the cracks in the concrete around the window frame.

Inspired by the claret, or the Sauternes, or even by the flies, Archie pulled a £20 note from his wallet and invested it with Padraig on River Slaney to win, at the quite generous odds of 6-1. The good River duly obliged with a great leap over the last fence that would have done credit to one of the salmon said to inhabit its waters, and came in the winner by a good three lengths. Archie went off in the greatest good humour to collect the £130 or so he reckoned was due to him after the taxman had had his nibble. Padraig was less happy and greeted him with 'Would you just mind waiting till after the next race, please, sir?' Archie asked why. Padraig said nothing but made a meaningful gesture towards the bottom of his bookmaker's satchel, which was very thinly covered with notes, nearly all of them green, Irish and of the £1 variety. Archie took the point and reckoned that nonetheless he could run to a bottle of champagne, which we took in the bar overlooking the betting ring and Padraig.

On the next race Archie put a more modest fiver on something called Roaring Forties, which did not seem too keen on fences. It crashed heavily at the second to last; the jockey got up but the horse did not. A gentleman appeared wearing the sort of trenchcoat the Stasi used to favour when they were in charge of East Germany. He also sported a bowler, which was not part of the Stasi uniform, and a revolver, which was. Two shots rang out and four more men appeared with long poles and a large roll of tarpaulin. Poor Roaring Forties was carried off on a makeshift catafalque, doubtless to turn up in due course some weeks later, in part at least, in those Boucheries Chevalines which somehow exist in the highstreets of the dingier French towns.

Archie, although slightly shaken by the experience, managed to make his way to Padraig, who had ten tenners in his fist. Would it be alright if the rest came in Irish pounds? Archie agreed that this would be fine and magnanimously waived any further calculation of the exchange rate.

The opera that evening was Montemezzi's *L'amore dei tre re*, once a great favourite at The Met but now virtually unperformed. Wexford at the time was going through its post-verismo, blood and thunder period of Italian opera, and the *Tre re* filled the bill admirably. Alas, the music was not much to Archie's taste, so the moment the curtain came down he proposed a drink.

This meant a short walk down Main Street to the Goal Bar, as it is named on the outside. To everyone within, and there were plenty of people within, it was Johnny Murphy's. We dropped into conversation with a man at our table on the usual 'Ah, you'll be over here for the opera' lines – not a very acute observation as Archie and I were still in our dinner jackets. This was followed by an enquiry on what we did to earn our daily bread. I replied that I was an opera critic and added, a little maliciously, that Archie was an opera singer. With his receding hairline, his cheeks reddened by the air of Wexford racecourse and his neatly trimmed silver goatee beard he was a natural. Our friend's eyes brightened behind his Guinness. 'I know. You're the fellow singing Archibaldo.' Like much of the rest of Wexford he had been to the dress rehearsal of *L'amore dei tre re* earlier in the week. Archibaldo was the name of the old blind king who booms away in vengeful tones for much of the evening. Archie, as he had to be known thereafter, was beginning to look uncomfortable. He spent many hours each year auditioning singers, but his own voice resembled that of a corncrake. Johnny Murphy's regular became cheerier and cheerier, while Archie's gloom deepened. 'The Singing Pubs Competition judges will be around any minute and I'm sure you'll give us a song.' It was time for defensive action. Just as journalists hate writing copy for which they are not going to be paid, I explained, so professional singers dislike performing when their contracts do not demand it. It didn't work. Our friend had a capture and he was not going to let it go. 'Back in a second', he shouted as he went off to the Gents to release some of the Guinness within him. 'We're off', said Archie, leaving several inches of his own stout undrunk in the glass.

Back in the bar of White's Hotel some of his composure

returned. No word of Archie's vocal prowess had reached here. It was 12.30 am and I announced that I had better go off and make a few notes on Montemezzi before bed. Archie suddenly remembered that his own room was a few miles off on the banks of the Slaney. He turned to Kevin, with whom we had been drinking, and asked whether by any chance he had a car. 'No', replied Kevin 'but I know a fellow who has.' We went out into White's car park and made towards a beetle-shaped Morris Minor of considerable age. Its colour was indistinguishable and its substantial covering of mud proclaimed it a real farming car. Kevin opened the rear door and revealed a body lying full length on the back seat. Very gently he rolled it half over and took the car keys from the righthand pocket. The body gave a slight grunt but otherwise appeared totally content. Kevin

and Archie drove off to the Slaney while I went to bed and Montemezzi.

'How did you get on?' I asked the next morning when I arrived to pick up Archie. The answer was 'Fine'. They had had another drink before parting company, and the body had accompanied Kevin back to Wexford. I opened the *Irish Times*, which has a proper sense of its priorities and puts its racing on Page 2 rather than hiding it away at the back, and there was a headline across six columns:

RIVER SLANEY FLOWS IN

'I think that deserves a pint of stout' was Archie's comment. The first of the day, before the flies upstairs had even woken up.

Members of the 1990 team pictured on the stage of the Theatre Royal. From left: Elaine Padmore, artistic director; Cyril Nolan, front-of-house manager; Barbara Wallace, chairman; Jerome Hynes, managing director; Ted Howlin, box-office manager; John Maher, bar; Stella O'Kennedy, costumes; Nicky Cleary, stage director; Ger Lawlor, local chorus manager.

Wexford of the Wonders – A Reminiscence

by Seamus Kelly

Seamus Kelly was drama critic of the Irish Times since 1945 and its daily columnist, Quidnunc, *from 1949 until his death in 1979. He believed that he had missed only one Wexford Opera Festival since 1951, and confessed that he couldn't understand how that happened, because he considered Wexford top among all the Festivals he has attended in many parts of the world during those years. He contributed this short recollection for the Festival's twenty-fifth year, 1976.*

Up to 1951 my friends in Wexford numbered exactly two, and one of them wasn't a Wexford man at all. He was the poet Padraic Fallon, a Galway man who was a Civil Servant in Wexford. The other was Eugene McCarthy of White's Hotel, and neither of them, as far as I knew, had the remotest interest in opera. With Paddy I talked about poetry and played poker, while the Eugene context was in lifeboats (he was a dedicated propagandist of the Lifeboat Service) and in rugby football (he was a dedicated propagandist of Seamus Kelly, namesake but no relation).

Still, it was Eugene who shanghaied me to my first Festival in the teeth of all scepticism. You know the line: 'What? Opera? In *Wexford?* Don't be absurd!' It was a general line at the time, and it is to the eternal credit of Tom Walsh, Des Ffrench, and the people of Wexford that it was to be triumphantly disproven.

For that first *Rose of Castile* in 1951 the optimistic founder-fathers hoped to get 200 subscribers to underwrite their costs. In the event they got 500, and from then on the Festival never looked back, though from time to time it sailed on perilously stormy seas. Tom Walsh and his colleagues set their sights high right from the start, and those original standards have been kept through fifty-five operas. All the way back to those early days, too, the Wexford Festival was a gold-mine of exciting discoveries. New singers, new directors, new designers made the Irish Festival a springboard towards the top, so that veterans of twenty-five Festivals today can recall hearing some of the very finest artists in Wexford while they were on the way up. Freni, Sciutti, Egerton, Evans, Vanzo are some of the names that come back to me. Of the operas themselves, I remember with special delight *L'Elisir D'Amore,* in, I think, 1952, *Don Quichotte* somewhere in the sixties, and *La Clemenza di Tito.*

I was on the side of the angels – and of my paper's Music Critic – in this one, though I remember some sour-puss writing in the *Irish Times* that the production 'would have been vocally unacceptable as an end-of-term performance in a provincial college of music.'

Well, you can't please all the people all the time, and I remember a fine brouhaha at the time *Albert Herring* was done. Here you had a fierce cleavage of opinion, one group defending Britten's opera to the hilt, others contending that if Wexford wanted to stage that sort of thing, Gilbert and Sullivan were both funnier and more singable.

All the old hands remember happily the spontaneous late-night singing in White's and the Talbot, when the stars let their hair down, and every journalist who ever went to Wexford remembers the brisk sparring matches with Dr Walsh during the morning press conferences in White's Coffee-Room. Tom was a sparkling fencer, and I feel that he enjoyed those morning battles as much as we did.

I remember spending a golden Wexford morning with Compton Mackenzie and his grandniece. We hardly talked of opera at all, but he said that in his opinion MacLiammóir was the best Hamlet since John Barrymore, and then, in an aside to the girl 'Your great-aunt Fay was Barrymore's Ophelia, my dear.' Later we got on to Ballet and the grand old man said 'Of course, your great-great-grandmother danced with Taglioni. . . .'

And it was Mackenzie, for all his loyalty to his own Scotland, that gave the Wexford Festival one of its greatest accolades when he said publicly in 1967 'Wexford is a much better Festival than Edinburgh'. Who am I to disagree?

Dr T J Walsh, KM (1911-1988)

Doctor Tom's final curtain

by Bernard Levin

Since his first visit to the Festival in 1967, **Bernard Levin** *has become one of Wexford's most ardent disciples. As well as his annual reports in* The Times, *he devoted to Wexford the final chapter of his 1981 book* Conducted Tour, *in which he visited his twelve favourite music festivals around the world, concluding: 'Tom Walsh, thirty years ago, little knew what he was starting. Or perhaps he did; perhaps he understood that the world needs such happiness if it is not to perish utterly, and divined a way to bring about . . . a festival of music and joy to refresh the spirits, brighten the sky and flavour the year.' His moving obituary appeared in* The Times *on 14 November 1988.*

We laid Tom Walsh in the earth on Friday, under a glorious Indian-summer sun, in the Barntown cemetery outside the town; that way he can sleep amid the soft green hills of his native County Wexford which he loved so much. After the requiem mass in his home church, the cortège formed up; we filled the street from side to side and end to end. Solemn robed figures walked immediately behind the hearse; easily mistaken for members of the Guild of Mastersingers, they turned out to be the entire borough council, in full fig.

The town band wasn't there; perhaps it had been wrongly thought insufficiently reverent for such an occasion. The Taoiseach, though, had sent a telegram. The flowers, piled up, made an Everest of beauty and farewell; the church was heady with their scents. We sang 'Abide With Me', and meant it.

Well, your man had done a lot for the place, starting by being born there, in 1911 (he missed his 77th birthday by a fortnight). He qualified as a doctor at Dublin University in 1944; he practised in the town from 1944 to 1955; from 1955 to 1977 he was the anaesthetist for the Wexford County Hospital. In 1951 he founded the Wexford Opera Festival, and was its director until 1966.

His worth and achievements were recognised; the University of Dublin made him first an hon MA, then an hon doctor of philosophy, then an hon doctor of literature. He was an hon fellow of the Faculty of Anaesthetists of Ireland, a fellow of the Royal Historical Society, a Knight of Malta, a freeman of Wexford (well, I should think so). He wrote a series of scholarly books on the history of opera; he was twice married and widowed; he is survived by his daughter and sister.

Facts, facts; useful things for charting the stops of life, and seeing who gets off or on; not much good at conjuring the actual man on the actual bus. That shall be my task this morning.

Tom died smiling. At least, I assume he did; he was certainly smiling when I saw him in Wexford Hospital a few days before the end. As a doctor, he could not deceive himself about his condition, and his colleagues did not try to bluff him. But there were no solemn farewells; solemn farewells were not much in his line, except, to be sure, operatic ones.

Wexford knew him as 'Doctor Tom', and would call him nothing else. He had retired from active practice a decade before, but until recently he would keep his hand in by slipping over to England to do an annual locum.

When his health began to fail, some way into 1988, we devised Operation Tomplot — 'we' being the group of friends who go, every autumn, to his festival. We lured him to Sussex, he all unsuspecting while we were hiding out in the hedges and ditches around him, togged up and ready to carry him off to Glyndebourne; the girls had dressed more beautifully than ever, for him. The Plot held: 'Bernard, you swindler!' he cried, as the whole gang crashed through the door. I had wondered mildly, and put the point to his daughter Victoria, what she would say if he asked why the tea-table was set for 15. 'We'll keep him out of the room,' she said, 'and anyway, Daddy wouldn't notice.'

It was perfect Glyndebourne weather that day; a cloudless sky, a breeze to cool it, the gardens beginning to recover from the devastation of the hurricane. In the interval, up on the roof-terrace, the Christies poured libations, in which we drank his health. Brian Dickie was of the company; he is now general manager of Glyndebourne, but in 1967 he had had the alarming task of stepping into Tom's shoes as director of the Wexford Festival.

The Glyndebourne meeting was a moving moment; George Christie, a man who inherited a festival and thereafter dedicated his life to it, stood beside Tom Walsh, a man who created one out of nothing, and lived to see its fame spread wide. Then we went back into George's Festival Theatre, for the rest of *Die Entführung;* of course it had to be Mozart for Tom, whose love for that composer was passionate and unwavering.

Not many men devote their lives to the selfless service of their fellows. Tom Walsh did it twice over as doctor and as man of music. 'Doctor' says all that is necessary for the first part, and if you think it doesn't, ask his patients in Wexford. But 'man of music' is a feeble phrase for what it encompassed in his case. He simply decided that the quiet little town of Wexford should have an annual operatic festival to which, in due course, the world would come. And the money? Tut; the ravens fed Elishah.

I often wish I had been living in Wexford at the time; I would have loved to watch the scene as he went about the town telling people of his plan, while the news went much faster about the town that Doctor Tom had gone mad. For consider: Wexford in 1951 was not only a quiet place, unheard of outside Ireland and hardly heard of ever inside; it was also savagely poor. The theatre hadn't been used as such for a century (some say two); moreover it would hold only 400 people, and anyway it was now a furniture repository.

The very Muses wrung their hands and wept at so forlorn a hope, but they didn't know Doctor Tom; the iron-clad principles of rectitude and honour that guarded his life were translated into an irresistible inclination to see his dream realised. The Wexford Opera Festival, with the weeping Muses engaged for the chorus as a token of forgiveness,

opened its doors on time; that was 37 years ago, and they haven't shut yet. *Si monumentum requiris, circumspice.*

On Sunday morning during the festival, Tom always kept open house for his friends. Now he was adamant that he would be there to preside as usual, even if his hospital bed had to be put on wheels and pushed all the way to Lower Georges Street; as the week went by, though, even he had to admit defeat. But when he did, he was even more adamant that the ritual would be kept to, even if our host was from home.

Tom's Catholicism was deep, tenacious and complete; he suffered great distress when his beloved daughter married out of the faith. But there was no estrangement, and he died full of joy in the knowledge that a grandchild was soon due.

He sought no fame, no fortune. He had got hold of the notion that he was on earth to tend the sick and spread the love of music, and he pursued both vocations with great diligence and no fuss. It pleased him, as it pleased all of us, that over the years Wexford had become noticeably better off; his festival brought a good deal of money into the town.

We returned, *en masse,* to the hospital, to see him for the last time; the group was almost identical to that of the Great Tomplot. The doctors wouldn't let us in all together, but said we could go in two by two, each pair strictly enjoined to stay only a few minutes. He had been wandering a little, but he was perfectly clear with us.

He fought on for another week; death would not have dared approach his bedside until the 1988 festival was over. Last Tuesday afternoon, he fell asleep, and in sleep he left us. We who knew him will keep his memory bright, forever in his debt for the joy and friendship he and his festival have given us. We are even more blessed by having known and loved a man of such goodness, wisdom, generosity and laughter. Doubt not that he feasts in Heaven this night, with Mozart on one side of him and Hippocrates on the other, and a glass of good red wine in his good right hand.

Repertoire
1951-1990

Year	Title	Composer	Year	Title	Composer	Year	Title	Composer
1951	The Rose of Castile	Balfe	1970	L'Inganno Felice	Rossini		Un Giorno di Regno	Verdi
1952	L'Elisir d'Amore	Donizetti		Giovedi Grasso	Donizetti	1982	Sakùntala	Alfano
1953	Don Pasquale	Donizetti		Lakmé	Delibes		Arianna a Naxos	Haydn
1954	La Sonnambula	Bellini		Albert Herring	Britten		L'Isola Disabitata	Haydn
1955	Manon Lescaut	Puccini	1971	Les Pêcheurs de Perles	Bizet		Grisélidis	Massenet
	Der Wildschütz	Lortzing		La Rondine	Puccini	1983	Hans Heiling	Marschner
1956	Martha	Flotow		Il Re Pastore	Mozart		La Vedova Scaltra	Wolf-Ferrari
	La Cenerentola	Rossini	1972	Il Pirata	Bellini		Linda di Chamounix	Donizetti
1957	La Figlia Del Reggimento	Donizetti		Oberon	Weber	1984	Le Jongleur de Notre-Dame	Massenet
	L'Italiana in Algeri	Rossini		Katá Kabanová	Janáček		Le Astuzie Femminili	Cimarosa
1958	I Due Foscari	Verdi	1973	Ivan Susanin	Glinka		The Kiss	Smetana
	Anna Bolena	Donizetti		The Gambler	Prokofiev	1985	La Wally	Catalani
1959	Aroldo	Verdi		L'Ajo nell'Imbarazzo	Donizetti		Ariodante	Handel
	La Gazza Ladra	Rossini	1974	Medea in Corinto	Mayr		The Rise and Fall of the City of Mahagonny	Weill
1961	Ernani	Verdi		Thaïs	Massenet			
	Mireille	Gounod		Der Barbier von Bagdad	Cornelius	1986	Königskinder	Humperdinck
1962	L'Amico Fritz	Mascagni	1975	Le Roi d'Ys	Lalo		Tancredi	Rossini
	I Puritani	Bellini		Eritrea	Cavalli		Mignon	Thomas
1963	Don Pasquale	Donizetti	1975	La Pietra del Paragone	Rossini	1987	La Straniera	Bellini
	La Gioconda	Ponchielli	1976	Giovanna d'Arco	Verdi		La Cena Delle Beffe	Giordano
	The Siege of Rochelle	Balfe		The Merry Wives of Windsor	Nicolai		Cendrillon	Massenet
1964	Lucia di Lammermoor	Donizetti		The Turn of the Screw	Britten	1988	The Devil and Kate	Dvořák
	Il Conte Ory	Rossini	1977	Hérodiade	Massenet		Elisa e Claudio	Mercadante
	Much Ado About Nothing	Stanford		Orfeo ed Euridice	Gluck		Don Giovanni Tenorio or The Stone Guest	Gazzaniga
	Corno di Bassetto	various		Il Maestro di Cappella	Cimarosa		Turandot	Busoni
1965	Don Quichotte	Massenet		La Serva e L'Ussero	Ricci	1989	Der Templer und die Jüdin	Marschner
	La Traviata	Verdi		La Serva Padrona	Pergolesi		Mitridate, Re de Ponto	Mozart
	La Finta Giardiniera	Mozart	1978	Tiefland	d'Albert		The Duenna	Prokofiev
1966	Fra Diavolo	Auber		Il Mondo Della Luna	Haydn	1990	Zazà	Leoncavallo
	Lucrezia Borgia	Donizetti		The Two Widows	Smetana		The Rising of the Moon	Maw
1967	Otello	Rossini	1979	L'Amore dei Tre Re	Montemezzi		La Dame Blanche	Boieldieu
	Roméo et Juliette	Gounod		La Vestale	Spontini			
1968	La Clemenza di Tito	Mozart		Crispino e la Comare	Ricci Brothers			
	La Jolie Fille de Perth	Bizet	1980	Edgar	Puccini			
1968	L'equivoco stravagante	Rossini		Orlando	Handel			
1969	L'Infedeltà Delusa	Haydn		Of Mice and Men	Floyd			
	Luisa Miller	Verdi	1981	I Gioielle Della Madonna	Wolf-Ferrari			
				Zaide	Mozart			

```
                1 0 0
    NIGHTS  AT  THE  OPERA
 WEXFORD  FESTIVAL  OPERA
        AN ANTHOLOGY
```

1951-1990

1951
1, 2, 3, 4 November

The Rose of Castile
Michael William Balfe

Queen Elvira of Leon	Maureen Springer
Donna Carmen	Angela O'Connor
The Duchess of Calatrava	Statia Keyes
Don Pedro	James G Cuthbert
Don Florio	James Browne
Don Sallust	Michael Hanlon
Louisa	Nellie Walsh
Pablo	Seamus Roche
Don Alvaro	Brendan Nolan
Manuel	Murray Dickie

Wexford Festival Chorus
Radio Éireann Light Orchestra

Conductor	Dermot O'Hara
Producer	Powell Lloyd
Prima Ballerina	Joan Denise Moriarty

1952
29, 30 October; 1, 2 November

L'Elisir d'Amore
Gaetano Donizetti

Adina	Elvina Ramella
Nemorino	Nicola Monti
Belcore	Gino Vanelli
Dulcamara	Cristiano Dallamangas
Gianetta	Patricia O'Keeffe

Wexford Festival Chorus
Radio Éireann Light Orchestra

Conductor	Dermot O'Hara
Producer	Peter Ebert
Designer	Joseph Carl

1953
28, 29, 31 October; 1 November

Don Pasquale
Gaetano Donizetti

Don Pasquale	Cristiano Dallamangas
Ernesto	Nicola Monti
Dr Malatesta	Afro Poli
Norina	Elvina Ramella
A notary	N.N.

Wexford Festival Chorus
Radio Éireann Light Orchestra

Conductor	Bryan Balkwill
Producer	Peter Ebert
Designer	Joseph Carl

1954
3, 4, 6, 7 November

La Sonnambula
Vincenzo Bellini

Amina	Marilyn Cotlow
Elvino	Nicola Monti
Rudolpho	Franco Calabrese
Teresa	Thetis Blacker
Lisa	Halinka de Tarczynska
Alessio	Gwyn Griffiths
A notary	Daniel McCoshan

Wexford Festival Chorus
Radio Éireann Light Orchestra

Conductor	Bryan Balkwill
Producer	Peter Ebert
Designer	Joseph Carl

1955 (A)
30 October; 1, 3, 5 November

Manon Lescaut
Giacomo Puccini

Edmondo	Kevin Miller
Chevalier des Grieux	Salvatore Puma
Lescaut	Marko Rothmüller
Geronte de Ravoir	Gwyn Griffiths
Manon Lescaut	Esther Réthy
Innkeeper	Geoffrey Clifton
Dancing master	Daniel McCoshan
Sergeant of the Royal Archers	Geoffrey Clifton
Lamplighter	Daniel McCoshan
A singer	Celine Murphy

Wexford Festival Chorus
Radio Éireann Light Orchestra

Conductor	Bryan Balkwill
Producer	Anthony Besch
Designer	Peter Rice

1955 (B)
31 October; 2, 4, 6 November

Der Wildschütz
Albert Lortzing

Count of Eberbach	Thomas Hemsley
The countess	Monica Sinclair
Baron Kronthal	John Kentish
Baroness Freimann	Elizabeth Lindermeier
Nanette	Celine Murphy
Baculus	Max Pröbstl
Gretchen	Heather Harper
Pancratius	Richard Day

Wexford Festival Chorus

Conductor	Hans Gierster
Producer	Anthony Besch
Designer	Peter Rice

1956 (A)
28, 30 October; 1, 3, November

Martha
Friedrich von Flotow

Lady Harriet	Gisela Vivarelli
Nancy	Constance Shacklock
Sir Tristram Mickleford	Gwyn Griffiths
Plunkett	Marko Rothmüller
Lionel	Josef Traxel
The sheriff of Richmond	Geoffrey Clifton

Wexford Festival Chorus
Radio Éireann Light Orchestra

Conductor	Bryan Balkwill
Producer	Peter Potter
Designer	Joseph Carl

1956 (B)
29, 31 October; 2, 4 November

La Cenerentola
Gioachino Rossini

Don Ramiro	Nicola Monti
Dandini	Paolo Pedani
Don Magnifico	Cristiano Dallamangas
Clorinda	April Cantelo
Thisbe	Patricia Kern
Angelina	Barbara Howitt
Alidoro	John Holmes

Wexford Festival Chorus

Conductor	Bryan Balkwill
Producer	Peter Ebert
Designer	Joseph Carl

1957 (A)
27, 29, 31 October; 2 November

La Figlia del Reggimento
Gaetano Donizetti

The Countess of Berkenfeld	Patricia Kern
Ortensio	Gwyn Griffiths
Sulpizio	Geraint Evans
Maria	Graziella Sciutti
Tonio	Mario Spina

Wexford Festival Chorus
Radio Éireann Light Orchestra

Conductor	Bryan Balkwill
Producer	Peter Ebert
Designer	Joseph Carl

1957 (B)
28, 30 October; 1, 3 November

L'Italiana in Algeri
Gioacchino Rossini

Mustafa	Paolo Montarsolo
Elvira	April Cantelo
Zulma	Patricia Kern
Haly	Gwyn Griffiths
Lindoro	Petre Munteanu
Isabella	Barbara Howitt
Taddeo	Paolo Pedani

Wexford Festival Chorus

Conductor	Bryan Balkwill
Producer	Peter Ebert
Designer	Joseph Carl

1958 (A)
26, 28, 30 October; 1 November

I Due Foscari
Giuseppe Verdi

Francesco Foscari	Paolo Pedani
Jacopo Foscari	Carlo del Monte
Lucrezia Contarini	Mariella Angioletti
Jacopo Loredano	Plinio Clabassi
Barbarigo	Philip Talfryn
Pisana	Ellen Dales

Wexford Festival Chorus
Radio Éireann Light Orchestra

Conductor	Bryan Balkwill
Producer	Frans Boerlage
Designer	Michael Eve

1958 (B)
27, 29, 31 October; 2 November

Anna Bolena
Gaetano Donizetti

Henry VIII	Plinio Clabassi
Anne Boleyn	Marina Cucchio
Jane Seymour	Fiorenza Cossotto
Lord Rochefort	Geoffrey Clifton
Lord Richard Percy	Gianni Jaia
Smeton	Patricia Kern
Sir Hervey	Philip Talfryn

Wexford Festival Chorus

Conductor	Charles Mackerras
Producer	Peter Potter
Designer	Michael Eve

1959 (A)
25, 27, 29, 31 October

Aroldo
Giuseppe Verdi

Arnoldo	Nicola Nicolov
Mina	Mariella Angioletti
Egberto	Aldo Protti
Briano	Trevor Anthony
Godvino	John Dobson
Enrico	Griffith Lewis
Elena	Elizabeth Bainbridge

Wexford Festival Chorus
Radio Éireann Light Orchestra

Conductor	Charles Mackerras
Producer	Frans Boerlage
Designer	Micheál MacLiammóir

1959 (B)
26, 28, 30 October; 1 November

La Gazza Ladra
Gioacchino Rossini

Fabrizio	Trevor Anthony
Lucia	Elizabeth Bainbridge
Giannetto	Nicola Monti
Ninetta	Mariella Adani
Fernando	Paolo Pedani
Gottardo	Giorgio Tadeo
Pippo	Janet Baker
Isacco	Griffith Lewis
Antonio	Julian Moyle
Gregorio	Dennis Wicks

Wexford Festival Chorus

Conductor	John Pritchard
Producer	Peter Potter
Designer	Osbert Lancaster

1961 (A)
24, 26, 28, 30 September

Ernani
Giuseppe Verdi

Ernani	Ragnar Ulfung
Elvira	Mariella Angioletti
Don Carlos	Lino Puglisi
Don Ruy Gomez di Silva	Ugo Trama
Don Riccardo	Connall Byrne
Jago	John Evans
Giovanna	Elizabeth Rust

Wexford Festival Chorus
Royal Liverpool Philharmonic Orchestra

Conductor	Bryan Balkwill
Producer	Peter Ebert
Designer	Reginald Woolley

1961 (B)
25, 27, 29 September; 1 October

Mireille
Charles Gounod

Mireille	Andrea Guiot
Vincent	Alain Vanzo
Taven	Johanna Peters
Ourrias	Jean Borthayre
Vincenette	Elizabeth Rust
Ramon	Franco Ventriglia
Clemence	Morag Noble
Ambroise	Denis Wicks
Andreloun	Laura Sarti

Wexford Festival Chorus

Conductor	Michael Moores
Producer	Anthony Besch
Designer	Osbert Lancaster

1962 (A)
21, 23, 25, 27 October

L'Amico Fritz
Pietro Mascagni

Fritz Kobus	Nicola Monti
Suzel	Veronica Dunne
Beppe	Bernadette Greevy
David	Paolo Pedani
Henezo Derick Davies	Derick Davies
Federico	Adrian de Peyer
Caterina	Laura Sarti

Wexford Festival Chorus
Radio Éireann Symphony Orchestra

Conductor	Antonio Tonini
Producer	Michael Hadji
	Mischev
Designer	Reginald Woolley

1962 (B)
22, 24, 26, 28 October

I Puritani
Vincenzo Bellini

Sir Bruno Robertson	Adrian de Peyer
Elvira	Mirella Freni
Lord Arthur Talbot	Luciano Saldari
Sir George Walton	Franco Ventriglia
Sir Richard Forth	Lino Puglisi
Lord Walton	Derick Davies
Queen Henrietta of France	Laura Sarti
Wexford Festival Chorus	
Conductor	Gunnar Staern
Producer	Peter Ebert
Designer	Reginald Woolley

1963 (A)
20, 22, 24, 26 October

Don Pasquale
Gaetano Donizetti

Don Pasquale	Guus Hoekman
Dr Malatesta	Dino Mantovani
Ernesto	Alfonz Bartha
Norina	Birgit Nordin

Wexford Festival Chorus
Radio Éireann Symphony Orchestra

Conductor	Antonio de Almeida
Producer	Michael Hadji Mischev
Designer	Anna Hadji Mischev

1963 (B)
21, 23, 25, 27 October

La Gioconda
Amilcare Ponchielli

Barnaba	Lino Puglisi
La Gioconda	Enriqueta Tarrés
La Cieca	Anna Reynolds
Zuàne	Derick Davies
Isèpo	Adrian de Peyer
Enzo Grimaldo	Giuseppe Gismondo
Alvise Badoero	Franco Ventriglia
Laura	Gloria Lane

Wexford Festival Chorus

Conductor	Gunnar Staern
Producer	Peter Ebert
Designer	Reginald Woolley

1963 (C)
27 October

The Siege of Rochelle
M W Balfe

Clara	Patricia McCarry
Captain Montalban	Martin Dempsey
Marquis de Valmour	Adrian de Peyer
Count Rosenberg	Brendan McNally
Michel	Derick Davies
Marcella	Anna Reynolds
The father guardian	Franco Ventriglia
First peasant girl	Angela Jenkins
Second peasant girl	Dorothy Wilson
Wexford Festival Chorus	
Pianists	Jeannie Reddin and Courtney Kenny
Producer	Douglas Craig
Designer	Reginald Woolley

1964 (A)
24, 26, 29, 31 October

Lucia di Lammermoor
Gaetano Donizetti

Lord Enrico Ashton	Lino Puglisi
Lucia Ashton	Karola Agai
Sir Edgardo	Giacomo Aragall
Raimondo Bidebent	Franco Ventriglia
Alisa	Laura Sarti
Lord Arturo Bucklaw	Alastair Newlands
Normanno	Edmund Bohan

Wexford Festival Chorus
Radio Éireann Symphony Orchestra

Conductor	Antonio de Almeida
Producer	Michel Crochot
Designer	Reginald Woolley

1964 (B)
25, 27, 30 October; 1 November

Il Conte Ory
Gioacchino Rossini

Il Conte Ory	Pietro Bottazzo
L'Ajo	Federico Davia
Isoliero	Stefania Malagu
Roberto	Walter Alberti
Un cavaliere	David Johnston
La Contessa Adele of Formoutiers	Alberta Valentini
Ragonda	Laura Sarti
Alice	Deidre Pleydell

Wexford Festival Chorus
Radio Éireann Symphony Orchestra

Conductor	Gunnar Staern
Producer	Peter Ebert
Designer	Reginald Woolley
Lighting	Francis Reid

1964 (C)
28 October; 1 November

Much Ado About Nothing
Charles V Stanford

Hero	Erica Bax
Beatrice	Soo-Bee Lee
Don Pedro	Noel Noble
Don John	John MacNally
Claudio	Dennis Brandt
Benedick	Richard Golding
Leonato	Herbert Moulton
Borachio	Edmund Bohan
Friar Francis	Frank Olegario
Dogberry	Frank Olegario
Seacole	David Johnston
Verges	Tony Daly

Wexford Festival Chorus

Conductor	Courtney Kenny
Producer	Peter Ebert
Designer	Reginald Woolley

1964 (D)
31 October

Corno di Bassetto
An entertainment devised by T J Walsh from the musical criticisms of Bernard Shaw

Bernadette Greevy
Franco Ventriglia
Jeannie Reddin
John Welsh

1965 (A)
23, 25, 28, 30 October

Don Quichotte
Jules Massenet

La Belle Dulcinée	Ivana Mixova
Don Quichotte	Miroslav Cangalovic
Sancho	Ladko Korosec
Pedro	Deidre Pleydell
Garcias	Christine Wilson
Rodriguez	David Johnston
Juan	Minoo Golvala
Ténébrun	Maurice Bowen
A bandit	Guiseppe Sorbello
First footman	James Armstrong
Second footman	Dermod Gloster

Wexford Festival Chorus
Radio Éireann Symphony Orchestra

Conductor	Albert Rosen
Producer	Carl Ebert
Designer	Reginald Woolley

141

1965 (B)
24, 26, 28, 30 October

La Traviata
Giuseppe Verdi

Violetta Valery	Jeannette Pilou
Dr Grenvil	Erich Vietheer
Marquis d'Obigny	Patrick McGuigan
Flora Bervoix	Gloria Jennings
Baron Douphol	Richard Golding
Gastone de Letorières	Philip Langridge
Alfredo Germont	Veriano Luchetti
Annina	Robin Bell
Giorgio Germont	Octav Enigarescu
Giuseppe	Dermod Gloster

Wexford Festival Chorus

Conductor	Gunnar Staern
Producer	Peter Ebert
Designer	Reginald Woolley

1965 (C)
27, 29, 31 October

La Finta Giardiniera
W A Mozart

La Marchesa Violante

Onesti	Mattiwilda Dobbs
Nardo	Federico Davia
Don Anchise	Francis Egerton
Arminda	Maddalena Bonifaccio
Serpetta	Birgit Nordin
Il Conte Belfiore	Ugo Benelli
Il Cavaliere Ramiro	Stefania Malagu

Radio Éireann Symphony Orchestra Players

Conductor	Gunnar Staern
Producer	Peter Ebert
Designer	Judith Ebert

1966 (A)
23, 25, 27, 29 October

Fra Diavolo
Daniel François Auber

Fra Diavolo	Ugo Benelli
Lord Cockburn	Antonio Boyer
Lady Pamela	Anna Reynolds
Lorenzo	Nigel Douglas
Matteo	Paschal Allen
Zerlina	Alberta Valentini
Giacomo	Enrico Fissore
Beppo	Renato Ercolani

Wexford Festival Chorus
RTE Symphony Orchestra

Conductor	Myer Fredman
Producer	Dennis Maunder
Designer	Reginald Woolley

1966 (B)
24, 26, 28, 30 October

Lucrezia Borgia
Gaetano Donizetti

Don Alfonso	Ayhan Baran
Lucrezia Borgia	Virginia Gordoni
Gennaro	Angelo Mori
Maffio Orsini	Stefania Malagu
Liverotto	Alan Morrell
Gazella	Wyndham Parfitt
Petrucci	Patrick McGuigan
Vitellozzo	Bruce Lochtie
Gubetta	James Christiansen
Rustighello	Francis Egerton
Astolfo	Gordon Farrell

Wexford Festival Chorus

Conductor	Albert Rosen
Producer	Frith Banbury
Designer	Reginald Woolley

1967 (A)
21, 23, 26, 28 October

Otello
Gioacchino Antonio Rossini

Othello	Nicola Tagger
Doge	Terence Sharpe
Iago	Walter Gullino
Rodrigo	Pietro Bottazzo
Lucio	Frederick Bateman
Elmiro Barberigo	Silvano Pagliuca
Emilia	Maria Casula
Desdemona	Renza Jotti
Gondolier	Frederick Bateman

Wexford Festival Chorus
Radio Telefís Éireann Symphony Orchestra

Conductor	Albert Rosen
Producer	Anthony Besch
Designer	John Stoddart

1967 (B)
22, 24, 27, 29 October

Roméo et Juliette
Charles Gounod

Juliette	Zuleika Saque
Stephano	Anne Pashley
Gertrude	Pamela Bowden
Roméo	Jean Brazzi
Tybalt	Dennis Brandt
Benvolio	Frederick Bateman
Mercutio	Henri Gui
Paris	Kenneth Reynolds
Grégorio	Terence Sharpe
Capulet	Jaroslav Horáček
Frère Laurent	Victor de Narké
Le Duc de Vérone	Richard van Allan

Wexford Festival Chorus

Conductor	David Lloyd-Jones
Producer	John Cox
Designer	Patrick Murray

1968 (A)
25, 28, 31 October; 2 November

La clemenza di Tito
Wolfgang Amadeus Mozart

Titus	Peter Baillie
Vitellia	Hanneke van Bork
Sextus	Maria Casula
Annius	Delia Wallis
Servilia	Elaine Hooker
Publius	Silvano Pagliuca

Wexford Festival Chorus
Radio Telefís Éireann Symphony Orchestra

Conductor	Theodor Guschlbauer
Producer	John Copley
Designer	Michael Waller

1968 (B)
26, 30 October; 1, 3 November

La Jolie Fille de Perth
Georges Bizet

Catherine Glover	Denise Dupleix
Mab	Isabel Garcisanz
Henri Smith	John Wakefield
Le Duc de Rothesay	Henri Gui
Ralph	Roger Soyer
Simon Glover	Silvano Pagliuca
Un seigneur	Maurice Arthur
Le majordome	Brian Donlan
Dancers	Alexander Roy
	Christina Gallea

Wexford Festival Chorus

Conductor	David Lloyd-Jones
Producer	Pauline Grant
Designer	Robin Archer

1968 (C)
27, 29, 31 October; 2 November

L'equivoco stravagante
Gioacchino Rossini

Gamberotto	Richard van Allan
Ernestina	Renza Jotti
Ermanno	Pietro Bottazzo
Buralicchio	Elfego Esparza
Frontino	Mario Carlin
Rosalia	Maria Casula
Conductor	Aldo Ceccato
Producer	John Cox
Designer	John Stoddart

1969 (A)
24, 26, 30 October; 1 November

L'infedeltà Delusa
Joseph Haydn

Vespina	Eugenia Ratti
Sandrina	Jill Gomez
Filippo	Alexander Young
Nencio	Ugo Benelli
Nanni	Eftimios Michalopoulus

Radio Telefís Éireann Symphony Orchestra

Harpischord Continuo	Mark Elder
Conductor	David Lloyd-Jones
Producer	John Copley
Designer	John Fraser

1969 (B)
25, 27, 29, 31 October; 2 November

Luisa Miller
Giuseppe Verdi

Count Walter	Silvano Pagliuca
Rodolfo	Angelo Lo Forese
Federica	Bernadette Greevy
Wurm	Eftimios Michalopoulos
Miller	Terence Sharpe
Luisa	Lucia Kelston
Laura	Enid Hartle
A countryman	Stephen Tudor

Wexford Festival Chorus

Conductor	Myer Fredman
Producer	John Cox
Designer	Bernard Culshaw

1970 (A)   *Double bill*
23, 26, 30 October; 1 November

L'Inganno Felice
Gioacchino Rossini

Isabella	Jill Gomez
Bertrando	Ugo Benelli
Ormondo	Robert Bickerstaff
Batone	Federico Davia
Tarabotto	Elfego Esparza

Giovedì Grasso
Gaetano Donizetti

The colonel	Federico Davia
Nina	Jill Gomez
Teodoro	Malcolm Williams
Sigismondo	Elfego Esparza
Camilla	Johanna Peters
Stefania	Janet Hughes
Ernesto	Ugo Benelli
Cola	Brian Donlan

Radio Telefís Éireann Symphony Orchestra

Conductor	David Atherton
Producer	Patrick Libby
Designer	John Fraser

1970 (B)
24, 27, 29, 31 October

Lakmé
Leo Delibes

Lakmé	Christiane Eda-Pierre
Malika	Yvonne Fuller
Ellen	Carmel O'Byrne
Rose	Angela Whittington
Mistress Benson	Gabrielle Ristori
Gerald	John Stewart
Nilakantha	Jacques Mars
Frederic	William Elvin
Hagi	Malcolm Williamson
Dancers	Lyn Walker, Anthony Bremner

Wexford Festival Chorus

Conductor	David Lloyd-Jones
Producer	Michael Hadji Mischev
Designer	John Fraser
Choreographer	Oenone Talbot

1970 (C)
25, 28, 31 October

Albert Herring
Benjamin Britten

Lady Billows	Milla Andrew
Florence Pike	Johanna Peters
Miss Wordsworth	Patricia Reakes
Mr Gedge	John Kitchiner
Mr Upfold	Patrick Ring
Superintendant Budd	Elfego Esparza
Sid	Alan Opie
Albert Herring	Alexander Oliver
Nancy	Delia Wallis
Mrs Herring	Enid Hartle
Emmie	Laureen Livingstone
Cis	Lillian Watson
Harry	Robin McWilliams

Conductor	David Atherton
Producer	Michael Geliot
Designer	Jane Bond

1971 (A)
21, 24, 26, 29 October

Les Pêcheurs de Perles
Georges Bizet

Leila	Christiane Eda-Pierre
Nadir	John Stewart
Zurga	Marco Bakker
Nourabad	Juan Soumagnas

Wexford Festival Chorus
Radio Telefís Éireann Symphony Orchestra

Conductor	Guy Barbier
Producer	Michael Geliot
Designers	Roger Butlin (set)
	Jane Bond (costumes)
	Robert Bryan (lighting)
Choreographer	Anthony Bremner

1971 (B)
22, 25, 28, 31 October

La Rondine
Giacomo Puccini

Magda	June Card
Lisette	Anne-Marie Blanzat
Ruggero	Beniamino Prior
Prunier	Alexander Oliver
Rambaldo	Thomas Lawlor
Perichaud	Brian Donlan
Gobin	Harold Sharples
Crebillon	Gavin Walton
Yvette	Sara de Javelin
Bianca	Susan Howells
Suzy	Myrna Moreno
A steward	Gavin Walton

Wexford Festival Chorus

Conductor	Myer Fredman
Producer	Anthony Besch
Designer	John Stoddart

1971 (C)
23, 27, 30 October

Il re pastore
Wolfgang Amadeus Mozart

Aminta	Anne Pashley
Elisa	Norma Burrowes
Tamiri	Anne Cant
Agenore	Richard Barnard
Allesandro	Eduardo Valazco

Conductor	Kenneth Montgomery
Producer	John Cox
Designer	Elisabeth Dalton
Continuo	Jean Mallandine

1972 (A)
27, 30 October; 2, 5 November

Il Pirata
Vincenzo Bellini

Ernesto	Marco Bakker
Imogene	Christiane Eda-Pierre
Gualtiero	William MacDonald
Itulbo	Noel Drennan
Goffredo	Hugh Richardson
Adele	Mary Sheridan

Wexford Festival Chorus
Radio Telefís Éireann Symphony Orchestra

Conductor	Leone Magiera
Producer	Michael Geliot
Designer	Jane Venables
Lighting designer	Robert Bryan

143

1972 (B)
26, 29, 31 October; 3 November

Oberon
Carl Maria von Weber

Oberon	John Fryatt
Titania	Louise Mansfield
Puck	Janet Hughes
Huon	Heikki Siukola
Gerasmin	Brent Ellis
Rezia	Vivian Martin
Fatima	Delia Wallis
Baibars	Michael Beauchamp
Haroun	Andre Page
Hakim	John Flanagan
A mermaid	Susan Lees

Wexford Festival Chorus

Conductor	Kenneth Montgomery
Producer	Anthony Besch
Designer	Adam Pollock
Lighting designer	Robert Bryan

1972 (C)
28 October; 1, 4 November

Kata Kabanová
Leoš Janáček

Savel Prokofjevic Dikoj	Jan Kyzlink
Boris Grigorjev	Ivo Zidek
Kabanicha	Sona Cervena
Tichon Ivanyc Kabanov	Patrick Ring
Katá	Alexandra Hunt
Vana Kudrjas	David Fieldsend
Varvara	Elizabeth Connell
Kuligin	Christian du Plessis
Glascha	Susan Lees
Fekluscha	Nellie Walsh

Wexford Festival Chorus

Conductor	Albert Rosen
Producer	David Pountney
Designers	Susan Blane
	Maria Bjornsen
Lighting designer	Robert Bryan

1973 (A)
25, 28, 31 October; 2 November

Ivan Susanin
M I Glinka

Antonida	Horiana Branisteanu
Vanya	Reni Penkova
Sobinin	William McDonald
Ivan Susanin	Matti Salminen
Sigismund	Colin Fay
Messenger	Dennis O'Neill
Russian warrior	Peter Forest
Dancers	Tessa Jarvis
	Anton Elder

Wexford Festival Chorus
Radio Telefís Éireann Symphony Orchestra

Conductor	Guy Barbier
Producer	Michael Hadji Mischev
Designer	Susan Blane
Lighting designer	William Bradford
Dance choreographer	Tessa Jarvis

1973 (B)
26, 30 October; 3 November

The Gambler
Sergei Prokofiev

Baboushka	Sona Cervena
The general	Joseph Rouleau
Pauline	Anne Howells
Alexei	Arley Reece
Blanche	Annabel Hunt
Marquis	Bernard Dickerson
Mr Astley	Richard Stilgoe
Nilsky	Dennis O'Neill
Potapitch	Peter Forest

Wexford Festival Chorus

Conductor	Albert Rosen
Producer	David Pountney
Designer	Maria Bjornson
Lighting designer	William Bradford

1973 (C)
27, 29 October; 1, 4 November

L'ajo nell'imbarazzo
Gaetano Donizetti

Il Marchese Giulio Antiquati	Manuel Gonzalez
Il Marchese Enrico	Suso Mariategui
Gilda Tallemanni	Silvia Baleani
Il Marchese Pippette	Bernard Dickerson
Don Gregorio Cordebone	Richard McKee
Leonarda	Johanna Peters
Simone	Richard Stilgoe

Wexford Festival Chorus

Conductor	Kenneth Montgomery
Producer	Patrick Libby
Designer	Adam Pollock
Lighting designer	William Bradford

1974 (A)
23, 25, 29 October; 1 November

Medea in Corinto
Giovanni Simone Mayr

Creusa	Eiddwen Harrhy
Creonte	Lieuwe Visser
Giasone	Arley Reece
Medea	Margreta Elkins
Ismene	Joan Davies
Egeo	William McKinney
Tideo	Robin Leggate
Evandro	Alexander Magri

Wexford Festival Chorus
Radio Telefís Éireann Symphony Orchestra

Conductor	Roderick Brydon
Director	Adrian Slack
Designer	David Fielding
Lighting designer	James McCosh

1974 (B)
24, 27, 31 October; 3 November

Thaïs
Jules Massenet

Palémon	Lieuwe Visser
Athanaël	Thomas McKinney
Thaïs	Jill Gomez
Le serviteur	Seán Mitten
Nicias	Francis Egerton
Crobyle	Helen MacArthur
Myrtale	Ann Murray
Albine	Ruth Maher

Wexford Festival Chorus

Conductor	Jacques Delacôte
Director	Jeremy Sutcliffe
Designer	John Fraser
Lighting designer	James Taylor

1974 (C)
26, 28, 30 October; 2 November

Der Barbier von Bagdad
Peter Cornelius

Nureddin	Kevork Boyaciyan
Bostana	Joan Davies
Abul Hassan Ali Ebn Bekar	Richard McKee
Margiana	Helen MacArthur
The Kadi Baba Mustapha	Francis Egerton
The Kalif	Antony Ransome
Muezzin I	Seán Mitten
Muezzin II	Michael Scott
Muezzin III	Harry Nicoll
A slave	Alexander Magri

Wexford Festival Chorus

Conductor	Albert Rosen
Director	Wolf Siegfried Wagner
Set designer	Dacre Punt
Costume designer	Alex Reid
Lighting designer	Jamie Taylor

1975 (A)
23, 26, 29, 31 October

Le Roi d'Ys
Edouard Lalo

Jahel	Michel Vallat
Rozenn	Christiane Chateau
Margared	Gillian Knight
Karnac	Stuart Harling
Mylio	Antonio Barasorda
Le roi	Juan Soumagnas
St Corentin	Juan Soumagnas

Wexford Festival Chorus
Radio Telefís Éireann Symphony Orchestra

Conductor	Jean Perisson
Director	Jean Claude Auvray
Designer	Bernard Arnould
Lighting designer	James McCosh

1975 (B)
22 (modern première), 25, 28 October; 1 November

Eritrea
Francesco Cavalli

Boreas	Ian Caddy
Iris	Jessica Cash
Alcione	Stuart Harling
Nisa	Anna Benedict
Itidio	James O'Neill
Eurimidonte	Philip Langridge
Dione	John York Skinner
Laodicea	Ann Murray
Misena	Jessica Cash
Eritrea	Anne Pashley
Theramene	Paul Esswood
Lesbo	Anna Benedict
Niconida	Ian Caddy
Argeo	Matteo de Monti

Wexford Festival Baroque Ensemble

Conductor	Jane Glover
Director	Ian Strasfogel
Designer	Franco Colaveccia
Lighting designer	James McCosh

1975 (C)
24, 27, 30 October; 2 November

La Pietra del Paragone
Gioacchino Rossini

Pacuvio	Ian Caddy
Aspasia	Joan Davies
Fabrizio	James O'Neill
Donna Fulvia	Iris Dell'acqua
Macrobio	Eric Garrett
Giocondo	John Sandor
Clarice	Sandra Browne
Asdrubale	Richard Barrett

Wexford Festival Chorus

Conductor	Roderick Brydon
Director	Adrian Slack
Production designer	John Bury
Continuo	Edward Lambert

1976 (A)
20, 23, 26, 29 October

Giovanna d'Arco
Giuseppe Verdi

Delil	Alexander Magri
Carlo VII	Curtis Rayam
Giacomo	Lajos Miller
Giovanna	Emiko Maruyama
Talbot	Arnold Dvorkin

Wexford Festival Chorus
Radio Telefís Éireann Symphony Orchestra

Conductor	James Judd
Director	Jeremy Sutcliffe
Designer	David Fielding
Lighting designer	Graham Large

1976 (B)
21, 24, 28, 31 October
27 October concert performance in Mr White's

The Merry Wives of Windsor
Otto Nicolai

Mistress Ford	Catherine Wilson
Mistress Page	Anne Collins
Mr Page	Ian Comboy
Slender	Keith Jones
Dr Caius	Seán Mitten
Fenton	Maurice Arthur
Falstaff	Michael Langdon
Mr Ford	Alan Opie
Townsman	Peter O'Leary
Ann Page	Sandra Dugdale

Wexford Festival Chorus

Conductor	Leonard Hancock
Director	Patrick Libby
Designer	Adam Pollock
Lighting designer	Graham Large

1976 (C)
22, 25, 27, 30 October

The Turn of the Screw
Benjamin Britten

The prologue	Maurice Arthur
The governess	Jane Manning
Flora	Victoria Klasicki
Miles	James Maguire
Mrs Grose	Margaret Kingsley
Quint	Lee Winston
Miss Jessel	Anne Cant

Wexford Festival Ensemble

Conductor	Albert Rosen
Director	Adrian Slack
Set designer	David Fielding
Lighting designer	James McCosh

1977 (A)
19, 22, 25, 28 October
24 October concert performance in Dún Mhuire Hall

Hérodiade
Jules Massenet

Phanuel	Alvaro Malta
Salome	Eilene Hannan
Hérode	Malcolm Donnelly
John the Baptist	Jean Dupouy
La jeune Babylonienne	Hilary Straw
Dancer	Clair Symonds
Hérodiade	Bernadette Greevy
Une voix	Bonaventura Bottone
Grand Pretre	Glyn Davenport
Vitellius	Michael Lewis

Wexford Festival Chorus
Wexford Children's Choir
Radio Telefís Éireann Symphony Orchestra

Conductor	Henri Gallois
Director	Julian Hope
Choreographer	Domy Reiter-Soffer
Designer	Roger Butlin
Lighting designer	John B Read

1977 (B)
20, 23, 26, 29 October
27 October concert performance in Dún Mhuire Hall

Orfeo ed Euridice
Christophe Willibald Gluck

Orfeo	Kevin Smith
Euridice	Jennifer Smith
Amor	Anna Benedict

Conductor	Jane Glover
Director	Wolf Siegfried Wagner
Choreographer	Domy Reiter-Soffer
Set designer	Dacre Punt
Costume designer	Alex Reid
Lighting designer	James McCosh

Wexford Festival Chorus
Members of the Irish Ballet Company

Artistic director	Joan Denise Moriarty

145

1977 (C)
21, 24, 27, 30 October

Il Maestro di Cappella
by Maffeo Zanon, based on music by Cimarosa

Il Maestro	Sesto Bruscantini

La Serva e L'Ussero
Luigi Ricci

Buontempo	Sesto Bruscantini
Marianna	Ruth Maher
Angelica	Carmen Lavani
Roberto	Bonaventura Bottone
Andrea	Michael Lewis

La Serva Padrona
Giovanni Pergolesi

Serpina	Carmen Lavani
Uberto	Sesto Bruscantini
Vespone	Angela Aguade
Conductor	James Judd
Director	Sesto Bruscantini
Designer	Tim Reed
Lighting designer	Jan Sendor

1978 (A)
25, 28, 31 October; 3 November

Tiefland
Eugene d'Albert

Nando	Bonaventura Bottone
Pedro	Jon Andrew
Sebastiano	Malcolm Donnelly
Marta	Mani Mekler
Tommaso	Alvaro Malta
Pepa	Carmel Patrick
Antonia	Aideen Lane
Rosalia	Caroline Tatlow
Moruccio	Pat Sheridan
Nuri	Dinah Harris

Wexford Festival Chorus (Chorus master: Alan Cutts)
Radio Telefís Éireann Symphony Orchestra

Conductor	Henri Gallois
Director	Julian Hope
Designer	Roger Butlin
Lighting	Victor Lockwood
Costume designers	Luke Pascoe
	Alison Meacher

1978 (B)
26, 29 October; 1, 4 November

Il Mondo Della Luna
Joseph Haydn

Ecclitico	Ugo Benelli
Four scholars	Peter O'Leary
	Gerard Delrez
	Graham Trew
	Greville O'Brien
Buonafede	Gianni Socci
Ernesto	Alan Watt
Cecco	Denis O'Neill
Clarice	Elaine Linstedt
Flaminia	Helen Dixon
Lisetta	Emily Hastings
Conductor	James Judd
Director	Adrian Slack
Set designer	Axel Bartz
Costume designer	Tim Reed
Lighting	Victor Lockwood
Continuo	Courtney Kenny

1978 (C)
27, 30 October; 2, 5 November
3 November (Prom performance)

The Two Widows
Bedrich Smetana

Karolina	Elizabeth Gale
Aneska	Felicity Palmer
Mumlal	Joseph Rouleau
Ladislav	Robert White
Lidka	Dinah Harris
Tonik	Bonaventura Bottone

Wexford Festival Chorus (Chorus master: Alan Cutts)

Conductor	Albert Rosen
Director	David Pountney
Designer	Sue Blane
Movement	Terry Gilbert
Lighting	Victor Lockwood

1979 (A)
24, 27, 30 October; 2 November

L'Amore dei Tre Re
Italo Montemezzi

Archibaldo	Alvaro Malta
Flaminio	Bonaventura Bottone
Avito	Neil McKinnon
Fiora	Magdalena
	Cononovici
Manfredo	Lajos Miller
Handmaiden	Colette McGahon
A young girl	Marie-Claire
	O'Reirdan
A young man	William Pugh
An old woman	Colette McGahon

Wexford Festival Chorus (Chorus master: Alan Cutts)
Wexford Children's Choir (Director: Sister Mary Walsh)
Radio Telefís Éireann Symphony Orchestra

Conductor	Pinchas Steinberg
Director	Stewart Trotter
Designer	Douglas Heap
Lighting	Graham Large

1979 (B)
25, 28, 31 October; 3 November

La Vestale
Gasparo Spontini

Cinna	Terence Sharpe
Licinius	Ennio Buoso
La Grande Vestale	Claire Livingstone
Julia	Mani Mekler
Le Grand Pontife	Roderick Kennedy
Un consul	Pat Sheridan

Wexford Festival Chorus (Chorus master: Alan Cutts)

Conductor	Matthias Bamert
Director	Julian Hope
Designer	Roger Butlin
Costume designer	Sue Blane
Lighting	Graham Large

1979 (C)
26, 29 October; 1, 4 November

Crispino e la Comare
Luigi and Federico Ricci

Don Asdrubale	Pat Sheridan
Contino del Fiore	Bonaventura Bottone
Crispino Tacchetto	Sesto Bruscantini
Annetta	Lucia Aliberti
Mirabolano	Gianni Socci
Fabrizio	David Beavan
Donna Giusta, La Comare	Ruth Maher
Bortolo	Peter O'Leary
A crier	Martin Shopland
Lisetta	Colette McGahon
Crispino's children	Eoin Colfer
	Deirdre Brogan
	Katherine Miller
	Fergal Coffey
Trumpeter	Seamus Mahony
Drummer	Jimmy Busher

Wexford Festival Chorus (Chorus master: Alan Cutts)

Conductor	James Judd
Director	Sesto Bruscantini
Designer	Tim Reed
Lighting	Graham Large
Continuo	Courtney Kenny

1980 (A)
22, 25, 28, 31 October

Edgar
Giacomo Puccini

Fidelia	Iris Dell'Acqua
Edgar	Nico Boer
Tigrana	Magdalena Cononovici
Frank	Terence Sharpe
Gualtiero	Roderick Kennedy

Wexford Festival Chorus (Chorus master: Kim Mooney)
Bride Street Boys' Choir (Director: Gerard Lawlor)
Radio Telefís Éireann Symphony Orchestra

Conductor	Robin Stapleton
Director	Roger Chapman
Designers	Douglas Heap (sets)
	Jane Law (costumes)
Lighting	Graham Large

1980 (B)
23, 26, 29 October; 1 November

Orlando
G F Handel

Zoroastro	Roderick Kennedy
Orlando	John Angelo Messana
Dorinda	Lesley Garrett
Angelica	Alison Hargan
Medoro	Bernadette Greevy
Conductor	James Judd
Director	Wilfred Judd
Designers	Kandis Cook (sets)
	Alison Meacher (costumes)
Lighting	Graham Large

1980 (C)
24, 27, 30 October; 2 November

Of Mice and Men
Carlisle Floyd

Lennie Small	Curtis Rayam
George Milton	Lawrence Cooper
Curley	John Winfield
Candy	Seán Mitten
Curley's wife	Christine Isley
Slim	Padraig O'Rourke
Carlson	Brendan Cavanagh
Ballad singer	Paul Arden-Griffith

Wexford Festival Chorus (Chorus master: Kim Mooney)

Conductor	John DeMain
Director	Stewart Trotter
Designer	John Cervenka
Lighting	Graham Large

1981 (A)
21, 24, 27, 30 October

I Gioielle Della Madonna
Ermanno Wolf-Ferrari

Maliella	Marie Slorach
Gennaro	Angelo Marenzi
Carmela	Nuala Willis
Rafaela	Carlo Desideri
Biaso	Brendan Cavanagh
Totonno	Harry Nicoll
Ciccillo	Philip Creasy
Rocco	Seán Mitten
Stella	Virginia Kerr
Serena	Marian Finn
Concetta	Nicola Sharkey

Wexford Festival Chorus (Chorus master: Simon Joly)
Bride Street Boys' Choir (Director: Gerard Lawlor)
Radio Telefís Éireann Symphony Orchestra

Conductor	Colman Pearce
Director	Graham Vick
Designer	Russell Craig
Lighting	Graham Large

1981 (B)
22, 25, 28, 31 October

Zaïde
Wolfgang Amadeus Mozart

Zaïde	Lesley Garrett
Gomatz	Neil Mackie
Allazim	Ulrik Cold
Sultan Soliman	Curtis Rayam
Osmin	Gordon Sandison
Conductor	Nicholas Cleobury
Director	Timothy Tyrrel
Designer	Dermot Hayes
Lighting	Graham Large

1981 (C)
23, 26, 29 October; 1 November

Un Giorno di Regno
Giuseppe Verdi

Cavaliere Di Belfiore	Donald Maxwell
Barone Di Kelbar	Sesto Bruscantini
Marchese Del Poggio	Lucia Aliberti
Giulietta Di Kelbar	Angela Feeney
Edoardo Di Sanval	Ugo Benelli
Tesoriere La Rocca	Gianni Socci
Conte Ivrea	Brendan Cavanagh
Delmonte	Tony Madden

Wexford Festival Chorus (Chorus master: Simon Joly)

Conductor	James Judd
Director	Sesto Bruscantini
Designer	Tim Reed
Lighting	Graham Large

1982 (A)
20, 23, 26, 29 October

Sakùntala
Franco Alfano

Sakùntala	Evelyn Brunner
Durvàsas	Richard Robson
Harita	Brian Kemp
A young hermit	Harry Nicoll
The king	David Parker
Anusuya	Rosamund Illing
Priyàmvada	Anita Terzian
The king's squire	Andrew Gallacher
Kanva	Armando Caforio
A fisherman	Brendan Cavanagh

Wexford Festival Chorus (Chorus master: Simon Joly)
Radio Telefís Éireann Symphony Orchestra

Conductor	Albert Rosen
Producer	Nicholas Hytner
Designer	David Fielding
Lighting	Mick Hughes

1982 (B)
21, 24, 27, 30 October

Arianna a Naxos
Josef Haydn

Ariadne	Bernadette Greevy

L'Isola Disabitata
Josef Haydn

Costanza	Bernadette Greevy
Silvia	Ursula Reinhardt-Kiss
Enrico	Philip Gelling
Gernando	Maldwyn Davies
Conductor	Newell Jenkins
Producer	Guus Mostart
Designer	John Otto
Lighting	Mick Hughes
Choreographer	Nigel Nicholson

1982 (C)
22, 25, 28, 31 October

Grisélidis
Jules Massenet

Alain	Howard Haskin
Gondebaut	Richard Robson
The prior	Christopher Blades
Marquis de Saluces	Sergei Leiferkus
Grisélidis	Rosemarie Landry
Bertrade	Joan Merrigan
The devil	Günter von Kannen
Fiamina	Rosanne Creffield
Little Loÿs	

Wexford Festival Chorus (Chorus master: Simon Joly)

Conductor	Robin Stapleton
Producer	Stephen Pimlott
Designer	Ariane Gastambide
Lighting	Mick Hughes

1983 (A)
20, 23, 26, 29 October

Hans Heiling
Heinrich Marschner

Hans Heiling	Sergei Leiferkus
The queen	Malmfrid Sand
Anna	Constance Cloward
Gertrude	Ingrid Steger
Konrad	Eduardo Alvares
Stephan	Richard Lloyd-Morgan

Wexford Festival Chorus (Chorus master: Simon Joly)
Radio Telefís Éireann Symphony Orchestra

Conductor	Albert Rosen
Producer	Stephen Pimlott
Designer	David Fielding
Lighting	Mick Hughes
Choreographer	Terry John Bates

1983 (B)
21, 24, 27, 30 October

La Vedova Scaltra
Ermanno Wolf-Ferrari

Monsieur le Bleau	Grant Shelley
Conte di Bosco Nero	Howard Haskin
Milord Runebif	Neil Jansen
Don Alvaro de Castille	Tom McDonnell
Arlecchino	Gordon Sandison
Rosaura	Jill Gomez
Marionette	Rosemary Ashe
Folletto	Christopher Adams
Pedro	Andrew Gallacher
Birif	Richard Lloyd-Morgan
Ladies	Marilyn Hunt
	Susan Lees
Conductor	Yan Pascal Tortelier
Producer	Charles Hamilton
Designer	Tim Reed
Lighting	Mick Hughes
Choreographer	Terry John Bates

1983 (C)
22, 25, 28, 31 October

Linda di Chamounix
Gaetano Donizetti

Maddalena	Jennifer Adams
Antonio	Brian Kemp
The Marquis di Boisfleury	Gianni Socci
The intendant	Brendan Cavanagh
Linda	Lucia Aliberti
Pierotto	Anita Terzian
Carlo	Ugo Benelli
The prefect	John O'Flynn

Wexford Festival Chorus (Chorus master: Simon Joly)

Conductor	Gabriele Bellini
Producer	Julian Hope
Designer	Annena Stubbs
Lighting	Mick Hughes

1984 (A)
24, 27, 30 October; 2 November

Le Jongleur de Notre Dame
Jules Massenet

Jean	Patrick Power
The prior	Christian du Plessis
Boniface	Sergei Leiferkus
A musician monk	John Cashmore
A sculptor monk	Richard Robson
A painter monk	Peter McBrien
A poet monk	Grant Shelley
A pardoner monk	Brendan Cavanagh
Man in the crowd and offstage voice	Richard Lloyd-Morgan
Two angels	Virginia Kerr
	Alexander Mercer
Martin	Tony Friel

Wexford Festival Chorus (Chorus master: Martin Merry)
Radio Telefís Éireann Symphony Orchestra

Conductor	Yan Pascal Tortelier
Producer	Stefan Janski
Designer	Johan Engels
Lighting	Mick Hughes
Choreographer	Terry John Bates

1984 (B)
25, 28, 31 October; 3 November

Le Astuzie Femminili
Domenico Cimarosa

Bellina	Susanna Rigacco
Romualdo	Peter-Christophe Runge
Filandro	Raul Gimenez
Giampaolo	Arturo Testa
Leonora	Nuala Willis
Ersilia	Nancy Hermiston
Conductor	Gyorgy Fischer
Producer	Andy Hinds
Designer	John McMurray
Lighting	Mick Hughes
Choreographer	Terry John Bates
Continuo	Courtney Kenny

1984 (C)
26, 29 October; 1, 4 November

The Kiss
Bedrich Smetana

Vendulka	Marie Slorach
Paloucký Otec	John Ayldon
Lukáš	Eduardo Alvares
Tomeš	Roger Howell
Martinka	Patricia Johnson
Matouš	Richard Robson
Barče	Nancy Hermiston
A frontier guard	Grant Shelley

Wexford Festival Chorus (Chorus master: Martin Merry)

Conductor	Albert Rosen
Producer	Toby Robertson
Designer	Bernard Culshaw
Lighting	Mick Hughes
Choreographer	Terry John Bates

1985 (A)
23, 26, 29 October; 1 November

La Wally
Alfredo Catalani

Wally	Josella Ligi
Stromminger	John O'Flynn
Gellner of Hochstoff	Ljubomir Videnov
Hagenbach of Sölden	Lawrence Bakst
Walter	Sunny Joy Langton
Afra	Jean Bailey
An old soldier	Richard Robson

Wexford Festival Chorus (Chorus master: Ian Reid)
Radio Telefís Éireann Symphony Orchestra

Conductor	Albert Rosen
Producer	Stefan Janski
Designer	Marie-Jeanne Lecca
Lighting	Mick Hughes
Choreographer	Terry John Bates

1985 (B)
24, 27, 30 October; 2 November

Ariodante
George Frideric Handel

Ariodante	Bernadette Greevy
Ginevra	Pamela Myers
Dalinda	Morag MacKay
Polinesso	Cynthia Clarey
Lurcanio	Raul Gimenex
The king of Scotland	Petteri Salomaa
Odoardo	Adrian Thompson

Members of Irish National Ballet
Members of Wexford Festival Chorus

Chorus master: Ian Reid

Conductor	Alan Curtis
Producer	Guus Mostart
Designer	John Otto
Lighting	Mick Hughes
Choreographer	Terry John Bates

1985 (C)
25, 28, 31 October; 3 November

The Rise and Fall of the City of Mahagonny
Kurt Weill

Leokadja Begbick	Nuala Willis
Trinity Moses	John Gibbs
Fatty the bookkeeper	Valentin Jar
Jenny Smith	Sherry Zannoth
Jimmy Mahoney	Theodore Spencer
Jack	Julian Pike
Bill	Richard Sutliff
Alaska-Wolf Joe	John O'Flynn
Toby	Brendan Cavanagh

Members of Wexford Festival Chorus

Conductor	Simon Joly
Producer	Declan Donnellan
Designer	Nick Ormerod
Lighting	Mick Hughes
Choreographer	Terry John Bates

1986 (A)
22, 25, 28, 31 October

Königskinder
Engelbert Humperdinck

King's son	William Lewis
Goose-girl	Daniela Bechly
Witch	Pauline Tinsley
Fiddler	Sergei Leiferkus
Wood-cutter	Curtis Watson
Broom-binder	Valentin Jar
Young girl	Kathleen Tynan
Innkeeper	John O'Flynn
Innkeeper's daughter	Roisin McGibbon
Stable-girl	Marijke Hendricks
City elder	Brian Donlan
Tailor	David Bartleet
Gatekeepers	Jonathan Veira
	Brindley Sherratt

Wexford Festival Chorus (Chorus master: Ian Reid)
Radio Telefís Éireann Symphony Orchestra

Conductor	Albert Rosen
Producer	Michael McCaffery
Designer	Di Seymour
Lighting	John Waterhouse
Choreographer	Terry John Bates

1986 (B)
23, 26, 29 October; 1 November
Also 4 November, Queen Elizabeth Hall, London

Tancredi
Gioacchino Rossini

Tancredi	Kathleen Kuhlmaan
Amenaide	Inga Neilsen
Argirio	Bruce Ford
Orbazzano	Petteri Salomaa
Isaura	Marijke Hendriks
Roggiero	Roisin McGibbon

Wexford Festival Male Chorus (Chorus master: Ian Reid)

Conductor	Arnold Oestman
Producer	Michael Beauchamp
Designer	William Passmore
Lighting	John Waterhouse

1986 (C)
24, 27, 30 October; 2 November

Mignon
Ambroise Thomas

Mignon	Cynthia Clarey
Wilhelm Meister	Curtis Rayam
Philine	Beverly Hoch
Lothario	Teodor Ciurdea
Laerte	Philip Doghan
Jarno	John O'Flynn
Frédérick	Joseph Cornwell
Antonio	John O'Flynn

Wexford Festival Chorus (Chorus master: Ian Reid)

Conductor	Yan Pascal Tortelier
Producer	Richard Jones
Designer	Richard Hudson
Lighting	John Waterhouse
Choreographer	Terry John Bates

1987 (A)
21, 24, 27, 30 October

La Straniera
Vincenzo Bellini

Alaide	Renata Daltin
Valdeburgo	Jake Gardner
Arturo	Ingus Peterson
Isoletta	Cynthia Clarey
Montolino	Mikhail Krutikov
The prior	Giancarlo Tosi
Osburgo	Philip Doghan

Wexford Festival Chorus (Chorus master: Roy Laughlin)
Radio Telefís Éireann Symphony Orchestra

Conductor	Jan Latham-Koenig
Producer	Robert Carsen
Designer	Russell Craig
Lighting	John Waterhouse
Choreographer	Terry John Bates

1987 (B)
22, 25, 28, 31 October

La Cena Delle Beffe
Umberto Giordano

Tornaquinci	Mikhail Krutikov
Calandra	Oliver Broome
Giannetto Malespini	Fabio Armiliato
Neri Chiaramantesi	Luis Giron May
Gabriello	Philip Doghan
Ginevra	Miriam Gauci
Fazio	David Barrell
Cintia	Kathleen Tynan
Lapo	Bruno Caproni
Doctor	Giancarlo Tosi
Lisabetta	Alessandra Marc
Trinca	Brendan Cavanagh
Fiammetta	Patricia Wright
Laldomine	Kate McCarney
A singer	Philip Doghan

Conductor	Albert Rosen
Producer	Patrick Mason
Designer	Joe Vaněk
Lighting	John Waterhouse

1987 (C)
23, 26, 29 October; 1 November

Cendrillon
Fairy tale in four acts by Jules Massenet
Libretto by Henri Cain, after Charles Perrault
(sung in French)

Pandolfe	Pierre-Yves Le Maigat
Madame de la Haltière	Joan Davies
Noémie	Jane Webster
Dorothée	Therese Feighan
Lucette	Claire Primrose
The fairy	Silvana Manga
Prince Charming	Robynne Redmon
The Master of Ceremonies	David Barrell
Dean of the Faculty	Brendan Cavanagh
The first minister	Patrick Donnelly
The king	Oliver Broome
The herald	Anthony Morse

Members of the Dublin City Ballet
Wexford Festival Chorus (Chorus master: Roy Laughlin)

Conductor	Stéphane Cardon
Producer	Seamus McGrenera
Designer	Tim Reed
Lighting	John Waterhouse
Choreographer	Terry John Bates

1988 (A)
20, 23, 26, 29 October

The Devil and Kate
Antonin Dvorak

Jirka	Joseph Evans
Kate	Anne-Marie Owens
Marbuel	Peter Lightfoot
Kate's mother	Joan Davies
A musician	Michael Forest
Children	Gavin Clare and Ross Dunphy
Lucifer	Marko Putkonen
Gatekeeper	Phillip Guy-Bromley
Hell guard	Geoffrey Davidson
Solo dancer	Julie Wong
The princess	Kristine Ciesinski
A chambermaid	Kathleen Tynan
The marshal	Alan Fairs

Wexford Festival Chorus (Chorus master: Roy Laughlin)
Radio Telefís Éireann Symphony Orchestra

Conductor	Albert Rosen
Producer	Francesca Zambello
Designer	Neil Peter Jampolis
Lighting	Paul Pyant
Choreographer	Terry John Bates

1988 (B)
21, 24, 27, 30 October
3 November, Queen Elizabeth Hall, London

Elisa e Claudio
Saverio Mercadante

Elisa	Lena Nordin
Claudio	Janos Bandi
Carlotta	Alice Baker
The Conte Arnoldo	Plamen Hidjov
The Marchese Tricotazio	Bruno de Simone
Silvia	Olga Orolinova
Celso	Philip Doghan
Luca	Marko Putkonen
Children	Donal and Evelyn Walsh

Wexford Festival Chorus (Chorus master: Roy Laughlin)

Conductor	Marco Guidarini
Producer	David Fielding
Designers	David Fielding
	Bettina Munzer
Lighting	Paul Pyant

1988 (C)   *Double bill*
22, 25, 28, 31 October

Don Giovanni Tenorio or *The Stone Guest*
Giuseppe Gazzaniga

Don Giovanni	Miroslav Kopp
Pasquariello	Balazs Poka
The commendatore	Norman Bailey
Donna Anna	Malmfrid Sand
Donna Elvira	Andrea Bolton
Maturina	Alison Browner
Duke Ximena	Joan Davies
Duke Ottavio	Finbar Wright
Biagio	Alan Cemore
Lanterna	Philip Doghan

Wexford Festival Chorus (Chorus master: Roy Laughlin)

Conductor	Simon Joly
Producer	Patrick Mason
Designer	Joe Vaněk
Lighting	Paul Pyant
Choreographer	Terry John Bates

Turandot
Ferruccio Busoni

Kalaf	Milan Voldrich
Barak	Balazs Poka
The Emperor Altoum	Norman Bailey
Turandot	Kristine Ciesinski
Adelma	Alison Browner
Truffaldino	Bruce Brewer
Pantalone	Alan Cemore
Tartaglia	Phillip Guy-Bromley
The queen of Samerkand	Malmfrid Sand
Dancers	Julie Wong
	Sarah Audsley

1989 (A)
26, 29 October; 1, 4, 10 November

Der Templer und die Jüdin
Heinrich Marschner

Maurice de Bracy	Paul Harrhy
Brian de Bois-Guilbert	William Stone
Rowena	Mary Clarke
Cedric	Björn Stockhaus
Wamba	John Daniecki
Oswald	Brian Bannatyne-Scott
Friar Tuck	Adrian Fisher
The Black Knight	Greer Grimsley
Locksley	George Mosley
Rebecca	Anita Soldh
Ivanhoe	Joseph Evans
Isaac of York	William Bankes-Jones
Lucas de Beaumanoir	Peter Loehle

Wexford Festival Chorus (Chorus master: Jonathan Webb)
Radio Telefís Éireann Symphony Orchestra

Conductor	Albert Rosen
Producer	Francesca Zambello
Designer	Bettina Munzer
Lighting	Kevin Sleep

1989 (B)
27, 30 October; 2, 5, 11 November
8 November, Queen Elizabeth Hall, London

Mitridate, Re de Ponto
Wolfgang Amadeus Mozart

Mitridate	Martin Thompson
Aspasia	Lena Nordin
Sifare	Cyndia Sieden
Farnace	Luretta Bybee
Ismene	Patricia Rozario
Marzio	Paul Harrhy
Arbate	Therese Feighan

Conductor	Marco Guidarini
Producer	Lucy Bailey
Designer	Peter J Davison
Lighting	Kevin Sleep
Continuo	Charles Kilpatrick

1989 (C)
28, 31 October; 3, 6, 12 November

The Duenna (Betrothal in a monastery)
Serge Prokofiev

Don Jerome	Neil Jenkins
Don Isaac Mendoza	Spiro Malas
The Duenna	Sheila Nadler
Don Carlos	Thomas Lawlor
Louisa	Amy Burton
Ferdinand	James Busterud
Antonio	Donald George
Clara	Paula Hoffman
The maskers	Brian Parsons
	William Rae
	Adrian Fisher
Lopez	Paul Arden-Griffith
Lauretta and Rosina	Yvonne Brennan
	Kathleen Tynan
Pedro	Andrew Forbes-Lane
Pablo	Robert Burt
Michael	Garrick Forbes
Father Augustine	Brian Bannatyne-Scott
Brother Elixir	John Daniecki
Brother Chartreuse	Geoffrey Davidson
Brother Benedictine	Björn Stockhaus
Monastery doorkeepers	Ian Baar
	Christopher Speight

Wexford Festival Chorus (Chorus master: Jonathan Webb)

Conductor	František Vajnar
Producer	Patrick Mason
Designer	Joe Vaněk
Lighting	Kevin Sleep
Choreographer	Terry John Bates

1990 (A)
25, 28 October; 1, 4, 9 November

Zazà
Ruggiero Leoncavallo

Zazà	Karen Notare
Cascart	John Cimino
Milio Dufresne	Claude-Robin Pelletier
Anaide	Ludmilla Andrew
Natalia	Theresa Hamm
Courtois	Keith Mikelson
Floriana	Yvonne Brennan
Bussy	Wojciech Drabowicz
Duclou	David Cumberland
Michelin	Nigel Leeson-Williams
Augusto	Brendan Cavanagh
Claretta	Constance Novis
Simóna	Elizabeth Hetherington
Madame Dufresne	Regina Hanley
Totò Dufresne	Laura Way
	Shirley Dempsey
Marco	Nigel Leeson-Williams

National Symphony Orchestra
Wexford School of Ballet and Modern Dance

Conductor	Bruno Rigacci
Producer	Jamie Hayes
Designer	Ruari Murchison
Lighting	Mark Pritchard
Choreographer	Terry John Bates

1990 (B)
26, 30 October; 2, 6, 10 November

The Rising of the Moon
Nicholas Maw

Brother Timothy	Francis Egerton
Danal O'Dowd	Gordon Sandison
Cathleen Sweeney	Pamela Helen Stephen
Colonel Lord Jowler	Lawrence Richard
Major Max von Zastrow	Peter-Christoph Runge
Captain Lillywhite	Keith Mikelson
Lady Eugenie Jowler	Pauline Tinsley
Frau Elizabeth von Zastrow	Annika Skoglund
Miss Atalanta Lillywhite	Marie-Claire O'Reirdan
Corporal of Horse Haywood	Max Wittges
Cornet John Stephen Beaumont	Mark Calkins
The widow Sweeney Lynch	Elizabeth Bainbridge
Gaveston	Thomas Lawlor
	Stephen Crook
Willoughby	David Buxton

Wexford Festival Chorus (Chorus master: Jonathan Webb)
Loch Garman Silver Band

Conductor	Simon Joly
Producer	Ceri Sherlock
Designer	Richard Aylwin
Lighting	Mark Pritchard

1990 (C)
27, 31 October; 3, 7, 11 November

La Dame Blanche
François Adrien Boieldieu

Gabriel	Panaghis Pagoulatos
Dikson	Antoine Normand
Jenny	Brigitte Lafon
Georges Brown	Jorge de Leon
Marguerite	Gillian Knight
Anna	Mariette Kemmer
Gaveston	Andre Cognet
MacIrton	David Cumberland

Wexford Festival Chorus (Chorus master: Jonathan Webb)

Conductor	Emmanuel Joel
Producer	Jean-Claude Auvray
Designer	Kenny MacLellan
Lighting	Mark Pritchard